ALL ABOUT ARRAN

BLACKIE & SON LIMITED
50 Old Bailey, LONDON
17 Stanhope Street, GLASGOW

BLACKIE & SON (INDIA) LIMITED
Warwick House, Fort Street, BOMBAY

BLACKIE & SON (CANADA) LIMITED
TORONTO

From an old engraving

Lochranza Bay

ALL ABOUT ARRAN

BY

R. ANGUS DOWNIE

BLACKIE & SON LIMITED
LONDON AND GLASGOW

All About Arran
First Published 1933

This reprint published 1999

The Banton Press
Isle of Arran
Scotland.

ISBN: 1 85652 163 X

First published, June, 1933
Reprinted, September, 1933
Reprinted, April, 1935

Printed in Great Britain by Blackie & Son, Ltd.,
at the Villafield Press, Bishopbriggs, Glasgow

To

Gordon Park

Tom Pettigrew

Fraser MacAllister

Jimmy Burr

PREFACE

When we were very young our parents took us year after year to Millport, on the island known as Cumbrae, in the Firth of Clyde. There were several factors which led them to choose this place, but to me its leading attraction was the entrancing view of Arran that it gave. On a clear morning we could see the peaks standing out against the blue sky, and the white-washed cottages of Corrie gleaming by the brink of the sea. And in broken weather the clouds would lie like a dingy blanket upon the heights until the wind blew them over, or the sun pierced them, and revealed the spire of Goatfell or the majestic figure of the Sleeping Warrior.

The sight always filled me with a feeling that had nothing to do with the ordinary processes of thinking, a longing inexpressible in words: a longing, moreover, that is quite inappeasable, for now, when I have explored the whole of that island, and clambered to the top of every one of those peaks, and know by sight at least the inhabitants of most of those cottages, a glimpse of its dark crest rising steeply from the water arouses it as keenly and namelessly as ever.

Preface

I have written this little book in the hope that it may be of interest and use to the many people who, like myself, suffer from Arran-mania, and to the many others who each year fall victims to that most delightful of diseases.

There exists a considerable literature about Arran; the bibliography of Dr. Tyrrell's *Geology of Arran* (1928) contains over a hundred and fifty items, not all in English. The books from which I have derived most pleasure and profit are *The Geology of Arran and the other Clyde Islands* by James Bryce (fourth edition, 1872), the two magnificent volumes of *The Book of Arran*, and Dr. Tyrrell's work. Other books consulted are explicitly named.

I wish to express my gratitude for permission to quote from the books named, to Viscountess Bryce (*The Flora of Arran*, by the late Viscount Bryce), Dr. G. W. Tyrrell and the Controller of H.M. Stationery Office (*The Geology of Arran*), Messrs. A. Guthrie and Sons, Ltd., Ardrossan (Landsborough's, *Arran, Its Topography, Natural History, &c.*), Messrs. H. F. and G. Witherby (*The Birds of the Island of Bute*, by J. M. McWilliam and *The Highlands with Rope and Rucksack* by E. A. Baker), and Messrs. Frederick Warne and Co. Ltd. (*Animal Life of the British Isles* by Edward Step). I am also indebted to the Scottish Mountaineering Club for permission to use the diagram of the climbs on the north face of Cir Mhor.

Wishaw *June*, 1933.

CONTENTS

Chap.		Page
I.	The Island of Arran	1
II.	The Growth of the Island	11
III.	Prehistoric Arran	20
IV.	Arran in History	34
V.	The Approach to Arran	47
VI.	Brodick to Lochranza	54
VII.	Along the West Coast	66
VIII.	Lagg to Brodick	76
IX.	Rambling and Scrambling	85
X.	Rock-Climbing in Arran	99
XI.	Animal Life	111
XII.	The Birds of Arran	120
XIII.	Flowers and Plants	133
Appendix I.	Place-names of Arran	143
,, II.	Distances, Walks, Golf-courses and Fishing	146
,, III.	List of Plants	148
Bibliography		159
Index		161

ILLUSTRATIONS

Page

LOCHRANZA BAY AND THE MANNER OF TAKING THE BASKING SHARK

A reproduction of an engraving from Thomas Pennant's *A Tour in Scotland and Voyage to the Hebrides*; MDCCLXXII. - - - *Frontispiece*

MAP OF ARRAN - - - - - - - - 3

DIAGRAM OF CLIMBS ON CIR MHOR - - - 105

CHAPTER I

The Island of Arran

Arran is part of the county of Bute, which also comprises the island of Bute itself, Inchmarnock, and the two Cumbraes, all situated in the Firth of Clyde. Arran has also two insular satellites in Pladda and Holy Isle. The area of Arran is about 165 square miles (106,149 acres, to be exact), and its coastline is about 60 miles long. In outline it roughly resembles a morning roll with two bites out of one side. To the east of it, some fifteen miles away, is the coast of Ayrshire, and to the west, across the Kilbrannan Sound, the long arm of Kintyre stands between it and the Atlantic. To the north is the mouth of Loch Fyne, and to the south the open sea. An important geographical feature which has had considerable influence upon the development of the island is its proximity to Ireland. The nearest point of Ireland is thirty-five miles away; but for more than half of the distance one is in the lee of Kintyre. The actual crossing from the Mull of Kintyre to Torr Head is only some thirteen miles.

For parochial purposes the island is cut in two by a line running from Lochranza in the north to near

Dippin Head in the south, dividing the eastern parish of Kilbride from the western parish of Kilmory.

The contrast between the rugged granite mountains of the northern half of the island and the undulating plateau and moorland of the southern half is very striking. The forest of peaks to the north, bewildering at first and always impressive, can upon mature consideration be divided into three groups: the Goatfell group, or the peaks within the semicircle formed by Glen Rosa, the Saddle, and Glen Sannox; the Cir Mhor group, stretching from Suidhe Fheargbas and the Castles in the north to Ben Nuis in the south; and the Ben Bharrain group, to the west and north of Glen Iorsa.

Goatfell, the highest peak, reaches 2866 feet. Cir Mhor, Ben Nuis, Ben Tarsuinn, Caisteal Abhail, Ben Bharrain, Cioch na h-Oighe, Am Binnein, Ben Chliabhain, and Ben Bhreac are all over 2000 feet. In the southern part the uplands form a plateau rather than ridges and peaks, and reach 1500 feet at one or two points.

Here it might be permissible to digress from geography towards spelling and pronunciation. In general I have followed the Ordnance Survey Map of Arran (scale: one inch to one mile) in the spelling of names. But I have continued to use Goatfell instead of Goat Fell, which is the O.S. usage. And on occasion I have not hesitated to follow other writers in the use of simpler forms—Ben Chliabhain, for example, instead of Beinn a' Chliabhain. This business of simplification can be carried too far,

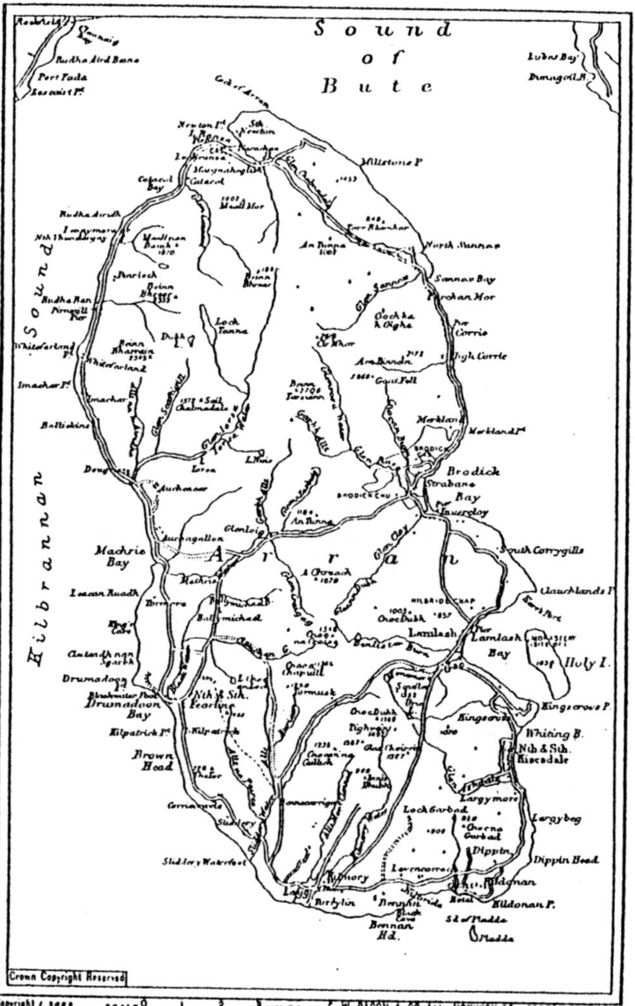

Copyright L.3089 SCALE 0 1 2 3 MILES G. W. BACON & CO. Ltd., NORWICH ST., FETTER LANE, E.C.

however. I admire the hardihood of those early travellers who wrote Ben Noosh for Ben Nuis (Bryce's Ben Ghnuis); but there is something in the appearance of *Noosh* that is scarcely Gaelic. Similarly no one with half an ear or half an eye would hesitate between Glen Rosa and Glen Rosie, both of which frequently occur.

On the other hand the purer Gaelic spelling of *The Book of Arran* is confusing to us Lowlanders. I am sure none of us care whether we write Lag or Lagg, Kilmorie or Kilmory; but Dubhgharadh and Ton-ri-gaoith for Dougrie and Thundergay call for too great an effort of memory.

The lack of obvious connexion between spelling and pronunciation leads us to suspect that Gaelic is a language that must be played by ear. The following are the generally accepted pronunciations of the common Gaelic names:

Cir Mhor,	Keer Vawr.
Ben Nuis,	B. Noosh.
Ben Tarsuinn,	B. Tarsoon.
Caisteal Abhail,	Ca-is-tel Avel.
Ben Bharrain,	B. Varen.
Cioch na h-Oighe,	Kioch na Oiche.
Ben Bhreach,	B. Vre-ak.
Suidhe Fhearghas,	Swi-e Fergus.

In pronouncing other Gaelic names the reader can do what I do, make a guess and hope for the best.

Of the glens the most important are Glen Rosa,

(K 656)

Glen Shurig, and Glen Cloy, converging on Brodick Bay: Glen Sannox, opening on to the tiny Sannox Bay; Glen Chalmadale and Glen Easan Biorach, issuing in fiord-like Loch Ranza; Glen Iorsa, the longest in the island; and, in the south, Glen Scorrodale and Glen Ashdale. The streams from which these glens take their names are not considerable in size; none of them is large enough to hold a canoe, for instance. But they form an intrinsic part of the landscape, and afford excellent fishing. Trout of a few pounds in weight are often hooked, sea-trout in their season, and an occasional salmon. The Machrie and the Iorsa Waters are the only streams on the island in which free fishing is not allowed. The largest loch is Loch Tanna, which is about a mile long and lies on the east side of Ben Bharrain, 1265 feet above sea level.

The most important human settlements are the small towns of Lamlash, Brodick, and Whiting Bay, facing the mainland. There are, besides, a number of villages all round the shore, Corrie, Lochranza, Pirnmill, Imachar, Dougrie, Machrie, Blackwaterfoot, Lagg, Kildonan, and the rest, and a number of scattered farmhouses.

Besides the road running round the island, following the coastline most of the way, there are two roads across the island: one, commonly called The String, from Brodick to Blackwaterfoot, and one from Lamlash by way of Monamore Glen and Glen Scorrodale to Lagg. Recently the surface and gradient of several parts of the main roads have been improved, and a few bridges have been widened. But even so it is hardly worth while to take a motor to the island, for the distances are not great, motors can be hired, and buses meet all steamers.

The climate of Arran is a happy compromise. "There is seldom" says *The Statistical Account of Scotland*, "any long continuance of intense heat in summer; and as seldom of extreme cold and frost in winter. Goatfell and the neighbouring hills are in winter usually covered with a mantle of snow. But on the lower grounds in the valleys along the coast, in the heaviest storms, snow seldom lies more than a day; and so rarely are there any severe visitations of frost and biting east winds, that at Arran Castle and the Whitehouse, many of the plants of warmer regions stand the whole winter in the open air. . . . It must be acknowledged, however, that what the island wants in snow and frost is abundantly made up to it in rain; of which few places even in the Hebrides receive a more liberal share. The prevailing winds are the south and the west, which almost always bring copious showers along with them. . . . Notwithstanding this superabundance of moisture, the climate upon the whole is far from being unpleasant. Those dull hazes and fogs, which often linger for days and weeks over many other places in this country, are in a great measure unknown in the parish of Kilbride; and days of constant rain do not often occur, mornings of drenching floods being not unfrequently succeeded by bright and beautiful afternoons of clear and smiling sunshine."

The last sentence should be underlined, for it describes one of the charms of the place. The frequent rain gives the landscape a continually fresh appearance, and prevents it from assuming that dry sunbaked aspect so wearingly monotonous to the traveller in the south. And the rarity of prolonged mist or rain is one point (not the only one) in which Arran excels Skye. The firm gabbro of its mountains attracts the mountaineer to Skye, and a certain literary glamour, derived mainly from Sassenachs like Dr. Johnson and H. V. Morton, draws many tourists thither. But one may spend a week, a fortnight, a month in Skye and scarcely have a dry day or a clear day. Such a thing is unheard of in Arran. All my holidays there have been spent under canvas, where one is naturally sensitive to the weather, and I have never had a holiday spoiled by rain.

In general the climate seems to be healthy enough. At the 1931 census there were upon the island 181 persons over seventy, 71 over eighty, and 21 over eighty-five. I remember conversing with a curious character, sent to Arran by a doctor in Girvan, who told him he was suffering from consumption. I offered my sympathy; but he assured me cheerfully that that was forty years ago. And when I saw him he looked as if his body would outlive his mind for many years to come.

The island derives most of its income from its summer visitors; but the industry which employs the greater number of its inhabitants is farming. Very little fishing is now done commercially. In the northern part, where the soil is poor, the methods and outlook of the farmers are not very advanced. Scrub bulls were the rule until they were prohibited by law, and rust is still seen in many a corn-field. At Ballickine, near Imachar, a form of the old runrig system, under which alternate ridges in a field belong to different people, is still maintained. On the other hand there are several excellent farms in the central and southern parts of the island.

Natural wood, principally alder, birch, hazel, rowan, and willow, grows along the west coast between Dougrie and Lochranza, on the east coast between Sannox and Brodick, and in the lower parts of several glens, such as Glen Cloy and Glen Rosa. Along the smaller streams, especially those with deep ravines, trees flourish up to 1000 feet; and to the east of the summit of the Corrie and Lochranza road there is a small forest at this height. On the north side of Glen Sannox one or two stunted rowan trees have struggled up to a height of 1500 feet. To the north of Brodick Bay, in the grounds of the Castle, there is an extensive plantation of fir. In general the southern part of the island is deficient in trees, though there are stretches at Lagg and along the banks of several of the streams.

At the census taken in April, 1931, the population of Arran, including the inhabitants of Holy Isle and Pladda, was 4532, which represents four people to every hundred acres. Of the inhabitants the *New Statistical Account* says: " In their persons, the people are generally tall; at least they are above the middle size, athletic, and very well made. Their features are open and regular, and their limbs remarkably well formed. The women are decidedly taller, handsomer, and better looking than in most parts of the country. These remarks apply generally to the whole parish, but they most particularly hold with regard to the south end of it. In their manners they are courteous and affable, having little of the awkward embarrassment which the Highland peasantry generally manifest in addressing strangers and superiors. In mind, they are distinguished for their sound sense, intelligence, acuteness, and liveliness. In business they are active, enterprising and judicious." It would be impossible to improve upon such a gallant description, except to suggest that their business instincts are usually kept well in hand.

There has been so much coming and going between Arran and the mainland that it would be foolish to regard the island as the stronghold of any distinctive racial features. There are many "incomers" now permanently resident upon the island, and still more whose blood is mixed. Here, as elsewhere, Gaelic is dying out as the vehicle of everyday conversation, although many of the older natives speak and understand it. At the last census nobody speaking Gaelic only was recorded, but eight per cent of the inhabitants of Kilbride and twenty per cent of the inhabitants of Kilmory spoke Gaelic and English. In winter the inhabitants of the island display a well-developed social instinct, and meet freely at dances and card parties; but when summer and the letting season comes round again all friendly intercourse is dropped. Or at least so I have been told.

Sooner or later the visitor to Arran is certain to meet a band of tinkers. He should regard them with interest, for they are " inheritors through centuries of ancestral, vagrant qualities, descendants of the most ancient families of Scotland—of the vagrant tribes." Sometimes one comes across them singly, or in pairs, but usually they travel in families, nearly always with one child in arms and several more afoot.

Racially they seem to be very pure; they all have the same wiry frame, the same brownish hair, the same lean face and fine clean-cut nose, and the same deep-brown eyes. They make some sort of a living by collecting cast-off clothes, helping in the hay-fields, begging, and, I dare say, a night's poaching once in a while. Some of them play the pipes well. Sobriety and cleanliness are alike unknown to them, and their camping places are easily traced by the wealth of filthy rags that they leave lying about. Of necessity they are honest—living on an island has its handicaps.

Few of these tinkers are resident in Arran all the year round. Most of them have homes on the main-land or in Kintyre, where they spend the winter. But every spring brings them forth again to pursue their ancient calling upon the island. It is not for us to find fault; perhaps they too suffer from Arran mania.

CHAPTER II

The Growth of the Island

"The number of rock formations, sedimentary and plutonic, which are found within this limited space is truly remarkable, perhaps unparalleled in any tract of like extent on the surface of the globe; while the varied phenomena which they present in their mutual contacts and general relations to one another are of the highest import in theoretical geology." Thus wrote Dr. Bryce in his book on the geology of Arran. Later writers are only slightly less enthusiastic, for though the claims of Arran's more ardent admirers might be disputed, one can still maintain that it contains a fuller record of certain of the great Scottish formations than any other district of equal extent.

Adequately presented, the geological history of Arran would be an enthralling detective story. It would tell how the island was searched for clues, how the evidence was pieced together and theories formed to explain existing conditions, how the hammer and the microscope, the resources of physical and chemical science, hours of patient labour and moments of brilliant insight have all contributed to our present knowledge. In the following slight sketch I have attempted only to outline the geology of the island, omitting many a "perhaps" and "possibly", and thus giving an appearance of finality and certainty which further investigation and discovery may destroy. Those desiring to study the subject in greater detail I would refer to the books named at the end of this volume, and to the extensive bibliography given in *The Geology of Arran* by Dr. Tyrrell.

Geologists divide the history of the earth into four primary divisions or eras, known as the Archæan, the Palæozoic, the Mesozoic, and the Kainozoic. These eras are further subdivided into several periods, upon the names and definitions of which geologists are by no means agreed. From information derived chiefly from the study of the radioactive substances in rocks it is believed that the age of the earth is between 1600 and 3000 million years. The Archæan era ceased, and the Palæozoic began, some 600 million years ago, while the Mesozoic began some 180 million years ago, and the Kainozoic some 60 million years ago. These figures give an idea of the length of time during which geological action has been taking place.

The oldest rocks in Arran belong to the Archæan era, and were originally laid down as deposits of fine mud, sand, and gravel at the bottom of a sea which at that time covered most of Scotland. Subsequently, by pressure from above and heat from below, this deposit, thousands of feet deep in parts, was converted into rocks. In texture they vary from coarse and gritty to fine-grained and slaty. They now form an incomplete ring round the granite peaks of the northern part of the island, interrupted for three miles between Glen Sannox and Whitewater, near Corrie. They occupy the whole of the shore line from Loch Ranza to Dougrie, and in the district between Glenshant Hill and Whitefarland form an elevated plateau rising to over a thousand feet.

Next in age comes a narrow strip of rock that crosses the lower part of the valley of North Glen Sannox. From its resemblance to other rocks in the Highlands, it is thought to be of Arenig age, an early period of the Palæozoic era, and of volcanic origin.

Old Red Sandstone, which was originally laid down as a deposit in the Palæozoic era, stretches in a semicircle from the Fallen Rocks, on the north-east coast of the island, to Dougrie on the west coast. In general this formation consists of coarse conglomerates, red mudstones, and purplish or chocolate-coloured sandstones, to a depth in places of several thousand feet. While this was being deposited volcanic action took place, and in the conglomerates subsequently formed pebbles derived from the lava are common. This same cycle of volcanic action extended over the southern half of Scotland, and threw up those eminences now known as the Sidlaw, the Ochil, and the Pentland Hills.

Next in order, also in the Palæozoic era, come the Carboniferous strata, which form a narrow strip along the eastern coast, between the Cock of Arran and the Fallen Rocks, and short stretches elsewhere.

Carboniferous Strata

The Carboniferous formation derives its name and its importance from the coal measures it usually contains. In Arran it is represented by shales, sandstones, and limestones which are distinguished from all the other sedimentary rocks of Arran by the wealth of plant and animal fossils that they contain. Coal is also to be found, though not in quantities of commercial interest, and two centuries ago was being worked on the shore at the Cock Farm, in the very north of the island.

While the Carboniferous strata were being laid down on the bottom of the shallow sea that covered at least the southern half of Scotland, several outbursts of volcanic action took place which have left distinct traces in Arran. North of the Corrie schoolhouse, for a distance of 350 yards, there is a stretch of igneous rocks dating from this period and made up mainly of massive lavas. The volcanic action of which this is the result must have taken place early in the Carboniferous period, for the thick limestones on the beach to the north of Corrie were deposited subsequent to it.

During the millions of years in which all these rocks were being deposited the area now occupied by the island of Arran rose and fell repeatedly, forming at one time the floor of a shallow lagoon, at another time the bottom of a deep ocean. But before the next formation began to settle, action of a more violent nature had taken place. By some mighty cataclysm of which we can trace the results but cannot guess the cause or imagine the extent, the rocks that had already been formed were heaved up and twisted and broken so that the Carboniferous strata, instead of being even and of equal thickness, were much higher in some places than in others. Those parts which were above the level of the sea remained there so long that the action of heat and frost and wind and rain reduced them to a level. At one point, now to the north of the mouth of the Machrie Water, the whole of the rocks of the Carboniferous period, a total thickness of some 1300 feet, was worn down and the Old Red Sandstone laid bare before the area sank again and the next system of rocks began to form.

The next system is called the New Red Sandstone, with which we leave the Palæozoic era and enter the Mesozoic. These rocks, distinguished from the Old Red Sandstone by the fossils which they contain, form a coastal strip from Corrie to Brodick, and the greater part of south Arran, though here they are riddled with intrusive igneous rocks of later date. The lower strata of the formation are of sandstone and conglomerate, and were originally sands of the desert, while the upper strata, chiefly of shales and marls, present the appearance of aqueous deposits. The lower strata can be seen rising to a height of 200 feet above the sea near the south end of Holy Isle. Fine stretches of the upper division are exposed in the old sea cliffs around the southern and south-western coasts, and in the lower courses of the streams debouching on these coasts.

The rocks of the New Red Sandstone period, the

last on the island to be formed by submarine deposit, were in place a very long time before, in the Kainozoic era, violent volcanic action threw out lava which is still seen in the terraced hills of Antrim, Mull, and Morven, cast up the Coolins and Red Hills in Skye, and raised huge masses of granite which now form the peaks of Arran. We are sure of the sequence of events, because no particle of granite is found among the sedimentary rocks, conclusive proof that the granite was not there until after the sedimentary rocks had been formed.

A great circular boss of granite, some eight miles in diameter, occupies the greater and higher part of the northern half of the island. When this boss was first raised it was still covered by a dome of sedimentary rocks, which have since been removed by erosion.

The granite occurs in two varieties: one, of coarse grain and earlier in age, forms the exterior of the mass; while a fine-grained and newer variety occupies about fourteen square miles upon the west side of Glen Iorsa. The peaks to the east are all of the coarse granite, whereas the rounded hills to the west are of the fine variety. Usually the fine variety breaks up into small slabs, which often so entirely cover the surface of the ground that no solid rock is observable. The debris of this rock is nearly white in colour, while the decomposition of the coarse granite produces a coarse brown sand.

Besides the northern granite nucleus there are hundreds of intrusive dykes and sills of Kainozoic age throughout Arran, and, in the centre of the island, a large and complicated area of fragmental rocks with numerous igneous masses, known geologically as " the Central Ring Complex ". In many places later dykes have been intruded into the granite itself. The dykes have generally weathered away quicker than the granite, especially the coarse granite, and many irregularities, such as the V-shaped gap in the north ridge of Glen Sannox known as the Carlin's Leap, have thus been formed.

When all this volcanic action was over, Arran formed part of a high plateau which included most of Scotland. " Following Professor Gregory, we believe that Arran was first planed down to a gently undulating plateau which stood 2000 to 3000 feet above sea-level, and was trenched by one, or perhaps two, of the early consequent north-east to south-west rivers. After the establishment of this system the country was again elevated, with the opening of the north to south clefts across the granite, and the production of great tectonic valleys to east and west, isolating Arran from the mainland. The land must have remained stationary for a period long enough for the formation of a low plain of marine erosion, which was raised by a third movement into the ' thousand-foot platform '. During these movements the climate had gradually become colder, leading up to the Glacial Period which now supervened." (Tyrrell, *The Geology of Arran.*)

The thousand-foot platform mentioned is represented by the shoulder of that height running out towards the sea on the east side of Goatfell, and may be traced in several of the other northern peaks.

During the Glacial Period an immense sheet of ice coming from the north covered the Clyde region, moving without check over the low ground of Bute and the Cumbraes, but being divided and turned slightly aside by the high hills of Arran. The action of glaciers can be traced plainly in Arran: they carried boulders of granite beyond where the granite itself occurs, they covered the southern half of the island with a thick sheet of boulder clay, they deepened and widened the valleys, depositing heaps of earth, or " moraines ", as they are called, at their mouths, they carved out deep corries, and they left tell-tale scratches on some of the rocks they had passed over.

Subsequent to the Glacial Period the island has undergone elevation several times. Evidence of raised beaches can be found at different levels, from 25 to 100 feet. The twenty-five foot raised beach is a distinct and important feature in the coastline of the island, and is also to be seen on neighbouring islands and both sides of the Firth of Clyde. In several parts the road and houses are situated on this beach. " Nowhere is it more strikingly exhibited than on the shore between Brodick and Glen Sannox, where it forms a long level strip of meadows, which are bounded on the inner side by a line of sandstone cliffs, pierced by many ancient sea-worn cliffs half-concealed beneath luxuriant overhanging vegetation." (Tyrrell, *The Geology of Arran.*) The marine shells found upon it appear all to be of species now living in the adjacent seas, so that, geologically speaking, its elevation must have taken place quite recently.

The landslips at Fallen Rocks and at Scriden happened within historical times. The former has left large conglomerate blocks of Old Red Sandstone Age piled up to a height of 500 or 600 feet. The Scriden landslip covered a large area of the most northerly part of the island with large blocks of New Red Sandstone. These fell, it is said, some two hundred years ago, with a concussion that shook the earth and was heard in Bute and Argyllshire.

CHAPTER III

Prehistoric Arran

The man of the Old Stone Age, that mighty hunter and clever artist who chased the bison and the elk and drew their image upon the walls of his cave, does not appear to have found a congenial home in Scotland. Indeed the only relics we have of his presence are some traces of fire, bones cut by human hands, and one pointed implement, which were found in caves near Inchnadamff, in a remote part of Sutherland. In time the Old Stone age came to a close and was succeeded, somewhere about 3000 B.C., by the New Stone age. Between these two ages a series of races, intermediate in time and culture, have been distinguished, and of these traces have also been found in Scotland.

The New Stone age is the earliest to be represented in Arran. We really do not know much about the life and habits of man in that remote age. We should know a great deal less had his conception of a life after death not led him to make burial chambers much stronger and more permanent in structure than the abodes of the living. At one time or another all the surviving monuments of this age on the island have been excavated, and the results are set forth with admirable fullness and accuracy by Professor T. H. Bryce in *The Book of Arran.*

At the head of the Kilmory Water, on the slope above it, about six miles from the sea, and to the west of the hill Glas Choircin, is a great cairn of stones known as Carn Ban. In shape it is roughly rectangular: its total length is 100 feet and its average breadth 60 feet. Between the top of the cairn and the steep hillside above it an almost flat semicircular area some thirty feet in diameter is partially defined by stones rising from a few inches to two feet above the ground. Other stones, marking the limits of the cairn, stretch out to north and south from the extreme points of this semicircle. The largest stones of the series stand in the axial line of the cairn, and the space between them forms a portal into a burial chamber which was found to occupy the upper end of the cairn.

Behind these two stones was a conical stone on edge, upon which were three large horizontal flags, partly overlapping each other. A fifth flag was laid bare when the small stones that partly covered the chamber were cleared away. These five flags formed a roof to the chamber.

During the excavation of the site these flags were removed, and the contents and measurements of the chamber below were carefully noted. It was found to be eighteen feet long, nine feet high, and three feet wide on an average. The lower parts of the walls were formed of large flags or blocks, the upper parts of smaller pieces of rock, after the manner of a dry-stone dyke. Transverse slabs divided the trench-like space into four compartments.

The chamber was found quite full of earth and stones, but the only relics recovered were one flake of flint and another of Corriegills pitchstone. The drainage from the hill, which ran through the floor of the chamber, had dissolved and carried away all the bones that once had been interred there.

The Carn Ban is the best preserved of the chambered cairns in Arran, and shows in full many features which can only be traced or imagined elsewhere. Thus in the cairn crowning the ridge which lies across the valley of the Struey, on the farm of East Bennan, in the very south of the island, the south side has been extensively quarried, and all the roofing slabs and the upper section of its walls have been removed. In the structure popularly known as the Giants' Graves, upon a hill overlooking Whiting Bay from the south, the base of the cairn alone remains, rising to a height of about two feet. Two standing stones represent the semicircle. The chamber is open at the south end, and is now without a roof, although there is still a huge flag leaning against the western wall which must at one time have been a roofing stone.

The Torlin (Ordnance Survey, Torrylin) Cairn, in the fields to the east of the Kilmory Water where it joins the sea, appears to have been reduced in extent since it was built, and is roofless. The frontal semicircle, the portal, and the end stone of the chamber are all missing. As in several other cases, all the compartments except the innermost had been rifled at some earlier period, possibly by the Vikings. On the right bank of the Sliddery Water, about a mile and a quarter from the sea, on the high ground sloping down to the river, is a chamber of which little remains but the slabs marking its foundations, and a heap of stones sixteen feet across which may be the remains of a cairn.

The first of the Tormore Chambers, at the south end of Machrie Moor, may be seen some hundreds of yards below the road from Shisken to Machrie. No trace whatever is to be detected of any mound or cairn. The massive side walls still stand, and beside them are three large flat slabs which probably formed the roofing. The other Tormore Chamber lies about three-quarters of a mile almost due north of this one. The cairn and the semicircle have disappeared, the roof has been removed, and there now remain only the side stones embedded in the peat. Its dimensions are smaller than those of the other chambers. The Moinechoill (O.S. Monyquil) Cairn, near the farm of that name, has been largely removed in the reclaiming of the land round it, one side alone remaining. A single compartment of the chamber is now entire. There is no stone which can with certainty be described as part of the frontal semicircle, though there are a few flags which apparently were erected to mark the outline of the cairn. The Monamore Chamber, standing on the high moor less than a mile to the south of Monamore

Burn, and slightly more than a mile from Lamlash, differs from the others in that it gives traces of a portal leading into the chamber. Little is now to be seen of the cairn, and only the lower parts of the chamber are left.

The Sannox Chamber still retains a fragment of its cairn, but nothing of its frontal semicircle. The chamber is divided into three compartments, all of which had been rifled many years before they were excavated. About three-quarters of a mile to the north of Lamlash are two heather-covered cairns which are distinguished as Dunan Beag and Dunan Mor. The first is a large rectangular cairn, with a tall pillar stone close to its eastern edge. Dunan Mor, on the other hand, is nearly circular in shape. An interesting feature of the Dunan Beag Cairn is that it contains two chambers, one near the north, the other at the south end. The Dunan Mor Cairn is even more unusual, in that three chambers, disposed in a radial fashion, have been discovered within it, all greatly dilapidated. A white cairn at Tormore mentioned by early writers has disappeared except for two stones which now form part of the wall of an outhouse.

Such in outline are the structures which remain and which when complete must have resembled Carn Ban. But though Carn Ban affords us a valuable key to structural details, it is from the other less perfect chambers that we derive our knowledge of what they contained. The only relics found in Carn Ban, as we have seen, were a flake of flint and a flake of Corriegills pitchstone. The chamber of the East Bennan cairn gave up a portion of a round-bottomed, bowl-like vessel of black ware, besides a flake of Corriegills pitchstone. The Giants' Graves were found to contain large deposits of burnt bone broken into very small fragments, which had all the appearance of human bones burnt by cremation. Four arrowheads and three large flint knives or scrapers were also found, as well as small fragments of pottery. From the Torlin chamber, besides a flint scraper and a fragment of pottery, the bones of at least six persons and some animal bones were recovered. Part of a human thigh-bone (unburnt), a primitive bowl-like urn, and a knife-like implement of flint were found in the Sliddery chamber. Flint tools and fragments of pottery, as well as a polished and perforated stone hammer, were found in the first of the Tormore chambers, while in the second no relics of any importance came to light. The south chamber of the Dunan Beag cairn yielded some interesting finds. In the first compartment were the unburnt remains of two adult persons, lying in a doubled-up position. In the second chamber was another unburnt interment. A number of animal bones were present, also some fragments of flint, pitchstone, and pottery, and parts of a jet necklace. The fragments of pottery are evidently pieces of a small vessel of the beaker type. The chambers of the Dunan Mor cairn are greatly dilapidated; but fragments of burnt bone, portions of a large rude vessel of red pottery, a flint knife or scraper, and flint and pitchstone fragments were discovered in one of them.

All of the chambered cairns mentioned belong to a late part of the New Stone Age. It is dangerous to hazard a guess as to the approximate date. Early in the New Stone Age Britain became an island, so that Arran was twice removed from the developments which spread over the continent. The Stone Age usages would linger on, and may even have persisted down to the time of the Roman invasion. The British Museum authorities are satisfied that cremation was not introduced into Britain before 1000 B.C.: probably all the Arran interments took place centuries after that date.

The pottery found within the chambers does not differ greatly from the type which prevailed during the New Stone Age, and is practically identical with the Dolmen pottery of western France; but the beaker urn in the Dunan Beag chamber, like the beads found there, is part of a later culture, being characteristic of the Bronze Age. The flint instruments probably came from the Antrim coast, which could easily be reached by way of the Mull of Kintyre. The presence of the Corriegills pitchstone shows that the flint was scarce enough to make a substitute acceptable. The bones found in the Torlin chamber have been meticulously measured, and competent authorities agree that they belonged to short people, with long heads, narrow faces, and well-arched foreheads, people, moreover, who were nearly related to the builders of the Long Barrows, and were the northern outposts of a common Mediterranean stock.

The chambered cairns of Arran correspond to the long barrows of Wiltshire and other parts of England. Stones have been used instead of earth, a difference easily explained by the natures of the two countries. Both forms are found in Ireland. The frontal semicircle would not appear to be a regular or a common feature, though it is found in the Giants' Graves of Sardinia. The chambers themselves are varieties of the stone table or " dolmen " type of monument. The dolmen is one of the most widely distributed of prehistoric monuments; it occurs in the Sudan, Egypt, Tripoli, Tunis, Algeria, and Morocco, in India, Syria, Palestine, the Crimea, the Caucasus, and, among European countries, in Bulgaria, Spain, Portugal, France, Belgium, Holland, N. Germany, Denmark, Sweden, Norway, W. England, and Ireland.

The original source of the dolmens has been the subject of much investigation and conjecture. One interesting theory, which is not yet (and possibly never will be) generally accepted, locates the beginnings of all ideas in Egypt, and derives the dolmen from the " mastaba " type of early Egyptian tomb. The upholders of this theory maintain that the idea spread not gradually but rapidly, by direct colonization. According to one of them, the long barrow was " either the tomb of an Egyptian noble, or else it was the tomb of a member of a ruling group established by an Egyptian noble somewhere in western Europe, perhaps in England itself." (Perry, *The Growth of Civilization.*) Be that as it may, there can be no question of direct settlement in Arran, for the chambered cairns were built by people following a tradition of which at least one important part had been forgotten. In Arran the cairns were built in any direction, whereas in the mastaba graves and the long barrows the axis always points east and west.

Somewhere in the Ancient East the use first of copper and then of bronze was discovered. This knowledge was spread over Europe by a race which is quite distinct from the race which preceded it. The man of the Old Stone Age had a long head, and buried his dead in long barrows or cairns: the man of the Bronze Age had a broad head and buried his dead in more or less circular tumuli. The Bronze Age is supposed to have lasted from about 2000 B.C. to 500 B.C.; but Scotland, and above all Arran, had a chronology of their own.

At one time it was taken for granted that the Bronze Age people, in the manner of later invaders, entered this country as successful warriors who overcame the earlier inhabitants by the use of their superior weapons. But now it is generally accepted that in its earliest stages human society was peaceful, and that warfare developed as an accidental excrescence. There is ample evidence that men of the Stone Age and of the Bronze Age lived together, and that the older usages gave way gradually to the newer. Even within the limited area of Arran such evidence can be traced. The facts that the Dunan Beag cairn contained two chambers, and that the Dunan Mor is nearly circular, indicate a new influence making itself gradually felt.

In a cairn about half a mile west of Kilmory Water, on the farm of Clachaig (O.S. Clauchog) were found both a chamber such as was used by the men of the Stone Age and a cist. Only a portion remained of the chamber. When it was cleared of soil no less than fourteen skeletons were uncovered, some of men, some of women, and two of young children. A rough black clay vessel and a polished stone axe were also found. The cist, which had probably been inserted in the cairn long after its construction, was typical of the Bronze Age, being formed of four stone slabs enclosing a space about three feet long, two feet broad, and two feet deep, and having a large capstone.

There are many Bronze Age cists in the island: a complete list is given by Dr. Bryce. Their structural features underground do not vary; but in different places they are accompanied by different forms of monuments upon the surface. They occur in circular cairns, in mounds, or within the area of stone circles, but often there is no visible structure to mark the site, and sometimes, as at Clachaig, they form secondary interments in the chambered cairns.

Upon excavation the terraced heap known as *Ossian's Mound* at Clachaig farmhouse was found to cover two cists. In a cist at the site of a former cairn at Blackwaterfoot a fine bronze dagger blade and a gold fillet came to light. The fillet probably came from Ireland, for the alluvial gold in the Wicklow Hills was well known and extensively exported during the Bronze Age.

There is a large number of stone circles in Arran. Upon Machrie Moor alone there are eight. On the farm of Achangallon (O.S. Auchagallon), overlooking Machrie Bay, there is a fine circle consisting of fifteen blocks, with a diameter of forty-seven feet. Near the highest point of the Brodick and Lamlash road, to the left going south, there are four massive round-topped granite blocks which once formed part of a circle. These circles and others of the kind that have been excavated have been found to mark typical Bronze Age cists. One cist, presumably the earliest, occupies the centre of the circle, and sometimes others lie between the centre and the circumference.

Single standing stones or monoliths, of which there are many, have also been found to mark the position of a cist. The most impressive of these monoliths, that at Achencar (O.S. Auchencar), rises to a height of 15 feet 7 inches. The well-known standing stone across the road from Brodick School was doubtless part of a Bronze Age interment. It is impossible to say whether any of these stones are true monoliths: there can be little doubt that some of them at one time formed part of a complete circle.

The short cists that have been excavated have yielded flint instruments, which shows that in spite of their knowledge of bronze the short cist people were still using flint extensively. The pottery vessels found in these cists all belong to the so-called "food-vessel" type. No short cist in Arran or Bute has revealed an urn of the "beaker" type, so common in England and the east of Scotland. As this type is also lacking in Ireland, we may conclude that the Bronze Age culture was introduced into Buteshire from Ireland, or into both from the same source, which was not Britain. The jet necklace and the small beaker in the Dunan Beag chamber seem to point to a secondary interment at a much later date, when at length the beaker culture had penetrated to Arran from the east coast of Scotland.

The character of the interment varies in the short cists, burnt and unburnt bones occurring in cists otherwise identical. Only two very imperfect skeletons have been found, and from these it has been demonstrated that the builders were broad-headed, a finding which agrees with the majority of skulls recovered from the short cists throughout Scotland. Their owners were related to the Round Barrow people of England, though, as the distribution of the beaker shows, that relationship was not immediate.

Of cinerary urn interments, which were very fashionable in some parts during the latter part of the Bronze Age, only three instances have been traced in Arran. The Iron Age, so important elsewhere, does not appear to have left any permanent monuments unless the so-called "forts" belong to it. The name of forts is apt to mislead, for there is little doubt that these structures were used for domestic as well as for military purposes. The best-known is at Kings Cross Point. This fort is almost circular, measuring about thirty-six feet in diameter. The wall is some twelve and a half feet thick, and is constructed with an inner and outer casing of stones of considerable size. The space between is filled with rubble. Red sandstone occurs in this wall: apparently it was easier for its builders to transport red sandstone from Holy Isle than to work the Trappean rock upon which it is situated.

In north Glen Sannox, about half a mile north of the road and the same distance from the sea, is a fort in a fairly complete and well-preserved state, commanding an extensive view. The main wall, which encloses an area of about 120 feet by 95 feet, would appear to have been ten to fifteen feet thick when intact. Huts eight feet in length and five or six feet wide were built into the wall on the western side.

Glencloy Fort, to which the misleading name of Bruce's Castle is sometimes given, consists of a simple circular outline upon a mound right above the Cloy Burn, about half a mile up Gleann Dubh. At Corriecravie, quite near the coast, are the remains of a fort of circular shape, with a vallum ten to twelve feet in thickness and forty-five feet in diameter. It is built similarly to the fort at Kings Cross. When it was dug out, the bones of deer and pig, a piece of hæmatite iron ore, and the stone top of a quern were uncovered.

The largest fort on the island is upon the headland

that rises above Drumadoon Point. It occupies the entire summit, an area of nearly twelve acres. To seawards the cliffs are so steep as to be impregnable. Upon the landward side was a stout wall, once probably ten feet thick, but now, so much has it been quarried, a mere track of stones.

There are also a number of domestic sites of an unknown but remote age scattered over the island, but more particularly in the south and west parts. These are circular structures, usually having an opening towards the south or south-east, to which the term " hut-circles " has been applied. There is a group of these circles on Tormore Moss, doubtless the remains of ancient villages.

Other interesting relics of prehistoric origin are the signs known as cup-and-ring marks, which occur sometimes on boulders and sometimes on the native rock. Those on the Stronach Ridge, near Brodick, have been very accurately measured.

CHAPTER IV

Arran in History

Like the happy country that it is, Arran has no history of its own, no continuous record of strife and warfare, and more than once has chosen the (historically uninteresting) ways of peace while over the rest of Scotland the claymore was flourishing. The historian is constrained, therefore, to recount such facts as are known about its past, in sequence, and with as great a show of continuity as he can devise.

Arran emerges into history a part of the kingdom of Dalriada. The Romans must have seen the island; but they did not come and conquer it. In A.D. 498, at a time when Arthur was trying to rid England of the Saxons, Irish colonists had settled in considerable numbers along the west coast of Scotland. Before that date the inhabitants of Arran were probably Picts with a strong strain of Irish blood derived from earlier settlers. These early Irish were known as *Scots*, and from them our country derived its name.

A poem on Arran by an ancient Irish bard which occurs in the thirteenth century prose tale, called *Agallamh na Senorach*, reflects the attractions which drew many of the Irish thither. It begins in this manner:

Arran of the many stags,
The sea strikes against her shoulders,
Companies of men can feed there,
Blue spears are reddened among her boulders.

Merry hinds are on her hills,
Juicy berries are there for food,
Refreshing water in her streams,
Nuts in plenty in the wood.

By A.D. 575 the Irish had acquired an independent kingdom, Dalriada, which comprised the whole of what is now called Argyllshire, including Kintyre, Arran, Bute, Jura, half of Mull, and Iona. The capital of this kingdom was Dun-add, an isolated hill-fort on Crinan Moss, and its religious centre Iona, where Columba had founded his monastery about 565.

Columba was not the first Irish missionary to Scotland, for the colonists of the fifth century were at least nominally Christians, and were accompanied by missionaries. Ninian and Kentigern had already begun the work before Columba took it up, and in the life of St. Brendan it is recorded that he visited the Western Isles about 545, and founded a monastery called Aileach, and one in Heth. Heth is now accepted to be the island of Tiree, and it has been demonstrated that Aileach was almost certainly on Arran—hence the name of Kilbrannan, or church of Brendan. Upon the shoulder that rises above the hamlet of Kilpatrick at the south end of Drumadoon Bay, about 300 feet up, is the cashel or wall that enclosed the site of the monastery. Only the foundations of a single circular building now remain. Not far off were found five hut-circles, probably intended originally for the lay dependants attached to the monastery. This cashel and the name of the hill above it—Torr an Daimh, or the hill of the church—are the only memorials of one of the earliest outposts of Christianity in Scotland.

From Iona Irish Christianity spread through Scotland (or Alba as we should call it at that date), and beyond to Northumbria, whither Aidan went to establish the monastery of Lindisfarne. It was brought to Arran about 680 by St. Molios (Molaise, Molingus, or Lasrian), who, after the manner of the Celtic missionaries, inhabited a lonely cell on what has ever since been called Holy Isle.

Nothing is now to be seen of the monastery that he founded; but the rock cell in which he lived is still intact. A ceremonial stone and a well, which are both connected by tradition with the saint's name, stand not far from the cell.

St. Molios was one of the lesser stars in the galaxy of Irish missionaries. Like Columba he was of royal kin. His boyhood was spent in Dalriada; but he was sent to Ireland, then famous as a home of learning, to complete his education. Only during part of his career was he connected with Holy Isle, for we hear of him subsequently journeying twice to Rome, and upholding the Roman usages against those of the Celtic Church. He returned to Ireland and became Abbot of Leithgliun in Leinster. He died there on 18th April, 639 or 640, that day being sanctified to his memory.

Holy Isle retained sacred relics of the saint, and was closely associated with his name, and this doubtless led to the founding of a house of friars there many years after. Practically nothing is known of this settlement, except that it was on the slightly sloping ground on the inner side of the island, about a mile from the sacred cave, and that its founder was possibly the "good John of Islay", Lord of the Isles, who died in 1380.

The Norsemen or Vikings are the next to appear upon the stage. The exact date of their first entry is unknown: they probably penetrated peacefully as merchants long before they descended upon our islands and coasts in plundering murdering bands. They confined their settlements in the first instance to the north of Scotland and the Isles, where they mingled with the Celtic population. From the mixed race sprang a generation of formidable leaders.

The Annals of Ulster record that in 794 the islands of Britain, meaning thereby the Hebrides, were devastated by Norse invaders. In 795 Iona was plundered; Rechra (an island near Dublin) was burned; and Skye was pillaged. Iona was again plundered in 802 and in 806. Arran probably escaped these raids, for the invaders were after richer spoils than were offered by the poor cell of St. Molios.

But about the middle of the ninth century Harold the Fair-haired made himself king of Norway, and many of the more independent spirits, to whom all authority was unbearable, left Norway to find new homes in the west, or in Iceland. Sporadic raids became deliberate conquest and settlement.

Those widely neglected masterpieces, the Icelandic Sagas, relate for us some of the deeds of the Norsemen upon our shores. The history of the Norse settlements in the Orkneys, and of expeditions to other parts, is well and fully told in the *Orkneyinga Saga*. In the *Laxdaela Saga* we learn how Ketill Flatnose brought his ships to Scotland in 890, won for himself half of Scotland, and was treacherously murdered.

Arran—known in Norse as Herrey or Hersey—could not be expected to escape so extensive a movement, and various relics of their occupation have come down to us. At Kings Cross Point, just next to the fort, a Viking grave mound was excavated, in which were found calcined human bones, a slab of whalebone, articles of iron, fragments of bronze, and a bronze coin. The iron articles were rivets and nails—parts of the boat, undoubtedly, in which the dead Vikings were burned, for such was the picturesque Viking usage. The bronze coin is a valuable clue, for it bears the name of Wigmund, who was Archbishop of York from 837 till 854. Now in 867, when such coins were doubtless still in circulation, York was captured by Ivarr the Boneless, a mighty Viking warrior. A few years later he was with a host at Dumbarton. In the little coin at Kings Cross we seem to have a link connecting these two enterprises.

Near the south bank of the Blairmore Burn, Lamlash, another Viking grave was found, from which the remains of a sword and a shield were recovered. These relics correspond to types found in the grave mounds of Norway of the eighth or early ninth century, and " proclaim this to be one of the earliest, if not the very earliest, Viking grave mounds yet discovered in Scotland ". The Vikings also visited Holy Isle, and left Runic inscriptions, which have been variously deciphered, upon the wall of St. Molios's cave.

A more convincing proof of their continued residence on the island is to be seen in the place-names, many of which, such as Brodick, Sannox, and Ranza, are of Norse derivation.

For centuries the Norsemen kept their hold upon the islands and part of the mainland of Scotland; but at length the Scots began to assert themselves. William the Lion imposed his authority over part of the old Norse territories, and his successor, Alexander II, carried the work still farther. Alexander III, the next upon the throne, persisted in the policy of opposing the Norsemen. Hakon, seeing his western kingdom crumbling away, determined to make an effort to assert his claims, and in 1263 prepared a fleet.

This fleet sailed round the north of Scotland, down the west coast, round the Mull of Kintyre, and came to rest in Arran Sound, or Lamlash Bay. From there Hakon sent messengers to the Scottish king at Ayr, to discuss their differences. Hakon claimed all the isles on the west of Scotland; but Alexander would not admit his claim to Bute and Arran and the Cumbraes. In the end it became evident that agreement was not possible, and Hakon sailed off to defeat at the battle of Largs. That battle was not more than a skirmish; but it effectively demonstrated to Hakon that he could no longer assert his claims by force of arms. He sailed back to Lamlash on his way home, but never saw Norway again, for he fell ill at Kirkwall and died there. His successor sold the islands to the Scottish king for 4000 marks down and 100 marks yearly, and Arran thus became part of the kingdom of Scotland.

Ecclesiastically, Arran formed part of the Diocese of the Isles, and the teinds of Arran belonged to the Bishop of the Isles, whose See was created about 1134, while the Norsemen still prevailed. For many centuries the Diocese of the Isles was unconnected with Scotland, being subject first to the Archbishopric of Hamburg, and then to that of Trondhjem.

When the direct succession to the Scottish crown failed, and the Scots had to assert their independence of English rule by the sword, Arran played an important part. Robert Bruce, an exile from the country of which he was nominally king, spent the winter of 1306–7 with his comrades upon the island of Rathlin, off the Irish coast. Towards spring his right-hand man, the good James Douglas, became impatient for action, and suggested a descent upon Arran, which was then in English hands. His plan met with general approval.

Douglas and perhaps a dozen companions accordingly set off in a single galley, and made for Kintyre. From there they crossed over in the dark to Arran, probably coming ashore either at Machrie or Drumadoon Bay. Under cover of night, and guided by Sir Robert Boyd, they crossed the island and concealed themselves in the woods near Brodick Castle. The castle was occupied by Sir John de Hastings, one of the claimants to the Scottish crown, who was holding the island for the English.

Next morning Douglas and his band ambushed a number of men who were carrying provisions from boats in the bay to the castle, and put them to the sword. The garrison of the castle heard the tumult and came out to assist, but were soon driven back to the security of the castle walls. Laden with the goods they had won, Douglas and his men retired to the woody Glen Cloy.

Ten days later Bruce followed with three hundred men in thirty-three small galleys. He landed on the east coast, probably at Whiting Bay, and was led to the hiding-place of Douglas by an old woman. There is no evidence to support the popular story that Bruce captured Brodick Castle. Next day a Carrick man, Cuthbert by name, was sent to the mainland to see how things lay there.

Seeing a fire on Turnberry Point, a prearranged signal, Bruce and his small army set off for the

Ayrshire coast. They were met by Cuthbert, who was in despair. He had found nothing but discouragement, and had not been responsible for the fire seen by Bruce. The king was in a quandary, and was uncertain whether to go forward or to retire to Arran; but his impulsive brother, Edward, settled the matter by saying that nothing would send him to sea again. And so the die was cast, and Bruce's reconquest of Scotland begun.

Bruce visited Arran again when his years of warfare were over, probably drawn thither by the fine hunting which the island afforded. Such a visit took place in 1326, when six men were paid two shillings as wages for taking the king's yacht across to Arran. For services rendered to him while concealed in the island, Bruce gave the lands of Kilmichael, in Glen Cloy, to Fergus MacLouis or Fullarton in a charter dated 26th November, 1307. In spite of the efforts of the Hamilton family, the Fullartons have held part of this property down to the present century. In 1400 Robert III granted them the office of " Crowner " or coroner. A descendant of the family who held this hereditary office died in 1932.

Much of Arran's early history is confused. It was held by the mighty Somerled, the first Lord of the Isles, and formed a bone of contention between his sons Reginald and Angus after his death. At one time it seems to have formed part of the earldom of Monteith, for we find members of that family holding the title of Lord of Arran, and making grants of land on the island to the monks of Kilwinning.

But it was already the property of the Stewarts before 1371, and upon the accession of Robert II to the throne it became part of the royal domain, and has its place in the royal accounts. The Stewart kings were not neglectful of parental responsibilities, even to such sons as were born out of wedlock, and various gifts of land in Arran and Bute were made to left-hand members of the family. These Stewarts are represented to-day by the Marquis of Bute.

Being part of the king's land, Arran was open to attack from the king's enemies, and in the fifteenth century it often suffered at the hands of the " cursed invaders from Knapdale and Kintyre ". These afflictions continued, indeed, until James IV reduced the islands to a state of peace.

The English also played their part, for when the Earl of Lennox, during the troubled time of Mary's minority, brought a dozen ships from Bristol to fight against his own country, he raided and plundered in Arran, and utterly destroyed Brodick Castle. The castle has been aptly compared to a phœnix.

In 1467 Sir Thomas Boyd married Lady Mary, the eldest sister of the young king James III, and in order to maintain his great rank was given various grants. These included the royal lands in Arran, which were erected into an earldom. The first Earl of Arran had a short innings, for in the autumn of 1469 his family's power was broken, and he had to flee to England. He forfeited the island of Arran, which thereafter reappears in the royal accounts.

James, son of the first Lord Hamilton, was the

next to hold the title of Earl of Arran, and was granted it for the conspicuous part he played in the affair of the marriage of James IV with the Princess Margaret of England. From that date the island has been held, somewhat insecurely at times, by the Hamilton family. For centuries they ruled the island with absolute power. At the abolition of hereditary jurisdiction in 1747, the Duke of Hamilton claimed £3000 compensation for the Arran justiciarship, but was not allowed anything.

More than once Brodick Castle was seized from its legitimate holders and was burnt or had to be won back by force. In September, 1558, the Earl of Sussex "burned the hole Cantyre; from thens went to Arren and did the lyke there". In 1646 the Campbells raided Arran, and laid waste all Brodick and the land around. In April, 1652, Major-General Deane, holding the Scottish command for Cromwell, sent a detachment from the garrison at Ayr to occupy Brodick Castle, which was still faithful to Charles II. The action of the soldiers aroused such hostility on the island that a foraging party, on their way back to the castle, was attacked and annihilated. This skirmish is said to have occurred between South Sannox and Corrie.

The first Duke, on his death, left the estates burdened not only with his debts, but also with a heavy fine imposed by the Commonwealth Government. He was succeeded, on failure of male heirs, by his daughter, the Duchess Anne (1630–1716), to whom belongs the credit of keeping the family estates intact and clearing them of debt. She was a remarkable woman, and earned the gratitude of her Covenanting compatriots by sheltering many fugitives in the woods of Hamilton Palace after the rout of Bothwell Bridge, and interceding with Monmouth on their behalf. Here in Arran she devoted her efforts to the internal development of the island. She first began to make roads and, at a cost of £2913, 10*s.* 5*d.*, built a harbour at Lamlash.

Later in the same century (1766–80) John Burrel, who was appointed to improve the island during the minority of the seventh duke, laboured manfully at his task. He introduced improved methods wherever possible: by enclosing, draining, planting, working coal seams, opening quarries, and building roads and bridges.

Yet Arran remained one of the most backward parts of Scotland. A Glasgow merchant who made the journey thither in 1783, considered that " it's situation for trade is excellent, but the laziness of the people obligeth them to overlook that advantage, and were it not necessity they would not even plant their few potatoes, sow their oats, or venture a mile from their shore in search of their fish." Headrick, whose *View of the Island of Arran* was published in 1807, relates that " in this island we behold the first rude efforts of man towards the cultivation of the earth ". The runrig system then prevailed throughout, no rotation of crops was known, in the stables the horses frequently stood to their knees in mire, and the cows were sheltered in a room adjacent to that in which the people themselves lived. "I nowhere saw an absurdity which is frequent in many parts of the Highlands, viz. the cows lodged in the same apartment with the people," says Headrick. Even in 1874 W. Mitchell, in *A Fortnight in Arran*, speaks of barbarous looking huts: "In many there is only a but and a ben, where the one is the house and the other the byre." The ruling family were in large measure responsible for this backward state, for the cottars were not encouraged to improve their homes, and the deer, which roamed freely over the whole island, made extensive agriculture impossible.

For the rest, Arran has been undisturbed by several of the issues which elsewhere led to arms and the spilling of blood: we have no knowledge of sufferers for the Covenant in Arran, and an attempt to raise men there for Prince Charles Edward proved unsuccessful. The reigning Duke of Hamilton did not escape the mania for abolishing men to make way for deer or sheep, a hundred years ago; but the actual clearances seem to have been carried out with less harshness and direct cruelty than in many another part.

CHAPTER V

The Approach to Arran

There are several ways of reaching Arran, though the services are not so good as they might be, and on Glasgow holidays both trains and steamers are usually crammed beyond the limits of comfort.

The most direct route to Brodick, Lamlash, and Whiting Bay is by way of Ardrossan. Trains, of course, run between Glasgow and Ardrossan in connexion with the steamers. Upon a clear day the peaks of Arran are in sight before the train reaches Ardrossan. A score of artists have attempted to render the distant prospect of Arran from almost every point of the Ayrshire coast. Goatfell crops up in the work of Scottish painters, nearly as often as does Fujiyama in the art of Japan. The grandeur of the peaks is wild enough to awaken poetic feeling within the most prosaic of us, yet Burns spent most of his life within sight of them and did not so much as mention them. "As soon as I saw them," wrote Keats, " I said to myself, ' How is it they did not beckon Burns to some grand attempt at Epic ? ' " But Keats confined his own poetic efforts to the dumpy mass of Ailsa Craig.

The View from the Sea

Wordsworth saw the island from the water, probably during his tour of 1803, and was moved to write a sonnet, which is not one of his best:

Arran! a single-crested Teneriffe,
A St. Helena next—in shape and hue,
Varying her crowded peaks and ridges blue;
Who but must covet a cloud-seat, or skiff
Built for the air, or winged Hippogriff?
That he might fly, where no one could pursue,
From this dull Monster and her sooty crew;
And, as a God, light on thy topmost cliff.
Impotent wish! which reason would despise
If the mind knew no union of extremes,
No natural bond between the boldest schemes
Ambition frames and heart-humilities.
Beneath stern mountains many a soft vale lies,
And lofty springs give birth to lowly streams.

The midday steamer, a somewhat top-heavy affair, quite willing for a heave and a roll on the slightest excuse, makes straight across for Brodick, lying at the base of Goatfell. Brodick is connected by motors —the only form of public conveyance in Arran— with the north, west, and south of the island, and those making for Lochranza, Pirnmill, Machrie, Blackwaterfoot, &c., consequently disembark there. Leaving Brodick, the steamer skirts round the precipitous coast, past the tail-end of Holy Isle, into Lamlash, and from there through the narrow passage between Kings Cross and Holy Isle to Whiting Bay.

A more interesting way of reaching this part of

the island, commendable to those not in haste, is by the steamer which leaves Wemyss Bay, and which sails through the Kyles of Bute before approaching Arran. Its progress along the coast permits an incomparable view of Glen Sannox, with Cir Mhor at its head, the Devil's Punchbowl, and the nave-like ridge of which Goatfell is the spire.

This steamer stops at Brodick, Lamlash, and Whiting Bay, and remains at Whiting Bay some time before returning by the same route. Travelling by this steamer one can thus spend several hours ashore and return the same day. Experienced hill-walkers have been known to climb Goatfell from Brodick and catch the boat on its return; but I should not advise any tyro to attempt the feat. For myself, I am all against introducing the modern curse of hurry and rush to the mountains, for reasons both physical and moral.

Other steamers, some of which start from the Broomielaw in Glasgow, can be joined at Greenock or Gourock, and stop at Lochranza and Pirnmill on their way to and from Campbeltown at the south end of Kintyre.

Such are the sailings on week-days: on Sundays there are no facilities for reaching or leaving the island.

Throughout the summer months excursions are run from various ports on the Clyde to parts of Arran or all round it, thus affording ample opportunity to appreciate its seaward aspects.

Upon one occasion a number of us chartered a

yacht, *Sayonara* by name, and made the crossing under sail, with a steady north wind blowing. Arthur, who was at the wheel, lamented that the keel was not heavy enough to let him sail two boards under; but even with the discretion thus imposed upon us we made a rapid passage. My own task was, upon a certain signal, to apply my not inconsiderable weight to one or other of the ropes which hung so neatly down the mast. The wind played funny tricks with us as we came opposite the glens and dips in the hills; but in time we anchored safely in Lamlash Bay. I would advise those who intend to do likewise to choose an anchorage well clear of the steamer's course, else they might be unpleasantly rocked as it passes. Lochranza offers the only other good anchorage in Arran.

My most eventful crossing was made in a much frailer craft. One of the follies of my youth which I least regret was the buying of a collapsible canoe. The skin was of rubber and canvas, the deck of canvas, and the frame of wood. Its weight was about seventy pounds, and its length sixteen feet. When dismembered it packed into four parcels, which could be carried almost comfortably by two persons. On the water it rather resembled a kayak, since the occupant was seated upon the bottom of the craft, and wielded a double-bladed paddle alternately upon either side.

A canoe is usually regarded as uncertain and easily capsized; but I should not allow anyone to say such things about mine. The roughest rapids and the heaviest seas it rides like a cork, and the only time it was overturned was when a current like a millrace swept us round a corner under a tree overhanging the water. I have since covered greater distances—from Crianlarich down the Tay to the Tay Bridge, and from Inverness to Largs—but I have never spent quite such a strenuous day as when we crossed from Fairlie, on the mainland, to Arran.

My companion upon that voyage was a cheerful youth of six feet or so, who refused to be impressed by the fact that he had never been in a canoe before. We assembled the canoe upon the shore at Fairlie, and then, after wading for quarter of a mile through shallow water and over nasty oyster-beds, stepped aboard. There was a fresh wind, but as yet no sign of rain. Overhead the sky was blue, and the Cumbraes, Arran, and Ailsa Craig stood out on the skyline as we made for Farland Point.

At Keppel Pier we were hailed by some friends who had been forewarned of our exploit. Rounding Farland Point into Kames Bay proved a ticklish job, for the wind was in the south-west, and kept blowing us towards the rocks. However we managed to land in Kames Bay, and went ashore in search of food.

When we resumed, the waves were larger than before, and the going much stiffer. Passing near the Tan Buoy we entered the channel used by the ocean-going steamers, and made for Garroch Head, at the south end of Bute. Upon a subsequent voyage, while on our way to Inveraray, a strong north wind made this passage impossible, and marooned us on the Lesser Cumbrae for three days. But the south-west wind, though steady, was not strong enough to hold us back, and a few hours of paddling brought us to Garroch Head.

We put in to land, but did not go ashore, as this part of the coast is very rocky. Hosts of gulls flew up noisily at our approach. On one point of rock was a young puffin. We spoke to him, and even touched him; but he merely looked indignant and went on with his toilet.

By this time the weather had changed and the rain clouds, which we had seen afar off over the peaks of Arran, were now upon us. For over an hour it rained fiercely, the big drops stinging our bare arms and utterly soaking our clothes. At this point, where two currents meet, the water is never quiet, and we had considerable difficulty in making any progress through the choppy waves, against the steady wind.

At length, as we left Bute astern, the rain stopped and the sun shone weakly out over the north of Arran. There was not enough heat in its rays to warm us, but continual exercise dried our bodies, leaving a thin rind of salt upon our arms.

The sun sank down beneath the hills, and the curtain of darkness descended as the short September day came to an end. Goatfell and Glen Sannox, the dark form of the Sleeping Warrior, and the white houses of Corrie melted into the gloom. We paddled blindly on until we distinguished tiny flickers of light. Our companions had come down in more orthodox manner, carrying the tent and stores, and had promised to light us a beacon if we had not appeared before dark. But this was no beacon. At first we thought it was a chink of light shining from under a door. After an hour it seemed to grow bigger: another hour and we made it out to be a window.

Alex's arms were cramping, and after each stroke he could straighten them only with a painful effort. My arms were only slightly sore; but the unusual position and exertion had brought on cramp in the stomach. For the last half-hour we paddled for two minutes and rested for three. Happily we were now in the lee of Arran, or the wind would have carried us helplessly out to sea again.

When we did reach land, after some ten hours of paddling, neither of us could stand steadily for a few minutes. We dragged the canoe over the rocks and left it on the front green of the house whose window light had guided us thence. Refusing kind offers of warm food, we set off for our camping-place, three miles away, in order to put the minds of our companions at ease about our safety. We arrived to find them all fast asleep. They were quite certain we would never get across, and in fact had eaten most of our food.

CHAPTER VI

Brodick to Lochranza

The steamer swings into Brodick Bay, and draws up at the pier. Ropes are thrown and made fast, gangways are laid down, and in a fury of unreasoning impatience we surge towards them. Having struggled on to the pier, we hand tuppence to the damsel at the turnstile, and are allowed to set foot upon Arran. We thread our way through the cars and buses that connect Brodick with other parts of the island, and start to circle Brodick Bay. A road to the left, dark in the shade of many trees, leads off to Lamlash. We take to the right.

" In few places on this fair earth is there beheld so delightful a mingling of beauty and grandeur as in the near view of Brodick," writes Landsborough, in his *Arran* (Guthrie, Ardrossan), and at present we are in a mood to overlook both his exaggeration and his verbosity. " Grandeur you certainly expect; for these magnificent mountains are seen from afar, and form the greatest ornament of our western coast. But you are not prepared for the remarkable beauty and sweetness given by the rich clothing of wood on the mountain skirts, down to water's edge; nor for the fine effect produced by

Brodick Castle, rising in ducal grandeur amidst the embowering foliage of many venerable trees; nor for the solemnizing of the deep-retiring glen, winding along the Rosa, till it seems lost in the embrace of the approximating mountains."

The main part of Brodick lies about half a mile round the bay from the pier. Here there are several well-appointed shops, besides two banks, a post office, and at least two good tearooms. The road now leaves the shore, and runs inland for a little. From this point a sandy beach stretches for a mile. Those who attempt a short-cut by keeping to the shore, as I did upon my first visit, will find their way barred by the Glenrosa Water. The grass-covered dunes form a golf course.

At the first cross-roads we turn to the right. The road to the left leads up Glen Cloy. In passing it might be said that Glen Cloy, and Glen Ormidale, and Gleann Dubh beyond, deserve at least one visit. Their attractions are on a smaller scale than those of Glen Rosa; but they are attractions, nevertheless, and are accessible with little effort from Brodick. Our road now runs parallel to the shore, with small white-washed cottages upon one side and the links upon the other until we approach the Glenrosa Water, where it again turns inland. If we were to follow it we should meet The String (as the road across the island is called), turn to the right over a hump-backed bridge, and pass one of the entrances to Brodick Castle. But nearly opposite the school, just before we come to the Standing Stone, we leave the road and take a short-cut across the golf links. We cross the river by a rickety bridge, skirt round a green, and follow the path along the edge of the fir plantation.

It is a place that to me always seemed haunted with a grace, a charm, a unity not to be defined or recaptured. There is a harmony in nature that cannot be represented by describing its single notes. Here the velvet green turf scattered with fir cones, that stretches down to the yellow sands and the restless blue sea beyond; the tall dark trees that sway in stately measure before the wind; the gorse bushes heavy with blossom that does not merely glow but blazes forth in purity and triumph, all blend with a hundred other features to form an enriching impression.

Our short-cut brings us out on to the road again below Brodick Castle.

Brodick Castle is the residence, for the greater part of the year, of the Duke and Duchess of Montrose. It has suffered both demolition and improvement during the course of its long history. It was demolished by the English in 1450, burnt in 1528, razed to the ground in 1544, and dismantled by the soldiers of the Commonwealth about 1646.

Part of the ground floor is built in a manner different from the rest of the building, and is thought to represent a part of the building destroyed in 1450. The larger staircase tower, the eastmost half of the main building, and the lower portion of the western half, may be attributed to the sixteenth century.

The small eastern tower and the battery are probably both of the seventeenth century. The more modern parts were built in 1844. The present castle is in the old baronial style, with steep crow-stepped gables, battlemented roofs, flanking turrets, and a lofty central tower. Inside, the only fixtures of any age are the old iron-studded oak doors.

Here it was that the first duke, when still only a marquis, entertained William Lithgow, the traveller, on his visit to Arran in 1628. The traveller spoke in high terms of the view from " Goatfield Hill "— " A larger prospect no Mountaine in the world can show, pointing out three Kingdomes at one sight: Neither any like Ile or braver Gentry, for good Archers, and hill-hovering Hunters."

On we go, past the old quay, the spot where Edward VII first trod Scottish soil after his coronation. For miles the road winds along by the sea. If it is early in the year a duck and a drake fly out of almost every creek at our approach. The rhododendron-covered bank upon our left, which has hitherto bounded our view, at length falls back, and we get a glimpse of the hills above. Three miles or so from Brodick we pass the abode of the gruffest-spoken, wildest-looking, kindest-hearted man in Arran.

Dozens of times, while camping on his ground, I have lain with the tent door open watching the lights twinkling on the mainland, probably with greater peace of mind than Bruce did six hundred years ago, or the sun rising in all its majesty over the low hills of Ayrshire. Sometimes, on a flying visit, we would neglect to take a tent, and slept in the hay—a form of luxury not to be shunned. One night the collie which usually slept with us did not appear, and we settled down without him. Although we had been climbing all day we did not get to sleep, for the rustling and scurrying in the hay, and an occasional scamper over our feet, kept us on edge. At two in the morning we decided to give it up, and carried our blankets out to a spot beside the road. We were all, I remember, somewhat originally dressed, after the manner of campers, and our blankets were of the same pattern as Joseph's coat. It was a perfect July night, without a breath of wind or a cloud in the sky. Overhead every star glittered as though newly polished, and I recollect thinking, as I lay on the brink of sleep, how perfectly apt was the French expression, *coucher à la belle étoile.* Campers only recapture half of the joy of him who sang of " a bed in the bush with stars to see ".

The lapping of the waves on the rocks soon hushed us to slumber. When we awoke the sun was high in the heavens. Carts, buses, cyclists, and pedestrians had been passing within a few feet of our heads for hours. I am told that our appearances were the subject of interesting discussions.

As we resume our way towards Corrie our eyes range north-east, to where the sun gleams on the beacon of Garroch Head and the lighthouse of the Little Cumbrae. Between the two we catch a glimpse of Millport. Directly north of us is the island of Inchmarnock, and the opening of the Kyles of Bute.

About a mile from Corrie we pass over the Water of Man. Upon each side of this burn, about a hundred yards from the road, is a boulder of granite, resting upon sandstone. The one on the north side —Clach Mhor, or the great rock—is the larger of the two, indeed the largest on the island. It is thirty feet square at the base, about fifteen feet high, and according to Dr. Tyrrell, must weigh about four hundred tons. Both of these boulders owe their positions to the agency of ice.

As we approach Corrie we cross the White Water. It is also called, in the Ordnance Survey, the Corrie Burn, but the other name is more suitable, since it describes it to perfection. The burn dashes down like a ribbon of white spray over the bare granite, and, especially after a heavy fall of rain, can be seen for miles out to sea. Sometimes when the peaks are overcast the White Water gleams like a stream issuing from the clouds.

From the bridge over the White Water we see the peak of Goatfell, with the shoulder running out towards us and terminating in Meall Breac, and the jagged ridge to the north which is called the Stacach. On the other side of the White Water, and much nearer to us, rises Am Binnein, a most uninteresting heap of granite that bears scarcely a blade of grass. Not far from the White Water, at a little distance from the road and hidden from sight, is the handful of houses that make up the clachan of High Corrie.

Corrie

On the outskirts of Corrie is the quay, which besides its more obvious function is often used for bathing, since the bottom is sandy and slopes gradually out to sea. There is a diving-board for swimmers only nearly opposite the hotel. The hotel is the only building of any size in the village, and can be seen for miles by those approaching from the south. Beyond the hotel is a stretch of white-washed cottages, and then the road bends suddenly to avoid the harbour. There is an old fishing boat lying rotting in the harbour to remind us of an industry once carried on much more extensively than at present by the natives. At one time Corrie exported a considerable quantity of limestone; the Crinan canal is constructed of Corrie limestone. Doubtless it was this trade which led to the construction of both the harbour and the quay.

Across the road from the harbour are the caves from which the limestone was quarried. These caves run into the hillside for a considerable distance. One of them appears now to be used as a joiner's workshop. To the north of Corrie, beyond the school, and at other points in the village, a number of new houses have been built. For many years "outsiders" were not encouraged to build on the island; but at present a more sensible, less exclusive policy prevails.

Corrie is my own choice among the villages of Arran, a choice obviously shared by the author of *Studies of Nature on the Coast of Arran.* Pirnmill and Machrie enjoy an hour or so more of sunshine each evening: Lagg and Kildonan escape some of the rain that falls here in the north-east: Brodick and Lamlash boast of their sands; and the partisans of Whiting Bay uphold the social superiority of the place. But Corrie has outweighing charms and conveniences. It lies at the foot of the hills, so much so that the houses are scattered along the thin strip beside the sea. There are no big new hotels or boarding-houses to spoil the artistic unity of its appearance, and as seen from a rowing-boat a hundred yards out, the tall dark ridge of Cioch na h-Oighe forms a perfect setting. The village, moreover, is used to climbers, and does not stare rudely at their old clothes or their heavily nailed boots.

The subject of male dress deserves a word in passing. Shorts can be worn in most parts of the island without arousing hilarity or sarcasm. In Lamlash shorts are tolerated, but in Whiting Bay they are definitely out of place. Only there need a holiday maker wear ordinary clothes. The kilt is becoming increasingly popular, and many who spend the rest of the year dressed like ordinary humans, at holiday time gird their hurdies in a swatch of tartan.

Between Corrie and the still smaller village of Sannox we pass several large blocks of granite. Beneath one of these, which lies three-quarters of a mile north of Corrie, a soldier of Cromwell is said to have hidden. This boulder is commonly called the "Cat Stone", a corruption of the Gaelic "Clach a Cath" or Stone of Battle. One story is that an Arran maiden ministered to his needs until they both escaped. Another tells how he was dragged forth and put to the sword. The second is probably the more accurate version: the first may be due to that feminine weakness, the desire for a happy ending. Quarter a mile nearer to Sannox is the Rocking Stone, which can be moved slightly by pressure applied from below.

We turn aside for a little to follow the rough road that leads up Glen Sannox. A few hundred yards from the main road we come to the graveyard. At one time, before the Reformation, a chapel stood upon the site; but little remains of it now except a sculptured stone, two feet three inches by one foot one inch, which is built into the outside of the surrounding wall. The rude effigy upon the stone is popularly believed to represent Saint Michael, to whom the chapel was dedicated. The chapel was probably connected with the Abbey of Kilwinning, to which Sir John Monteith granted the lands of Sannox and patronage of the churches in 1357. With morbid interest tourists invariably point out the grave of Rose, a young Englishman, who was cruelly murdered near North Goatfell in 1889.

The local families take turns in attending to the graveyard, and it is pleasant to remember that the place owes its neatness not to any commercial arrangement but to a true survival of communal spirit.

Beyond the graveyard are the workings of the barytes mine. This mine was originally opened in 1839, and was worked until 1862, when "the barytes mill, which marred the solitary grandeur of the scene which opens as we reach the plateau at the mouth of the glen, was entirely removed by order of the Duke of Hamilton ". In 1918 it was reopened, and in 1920 work was begun again in earnest. A new shaft was then sunk, and a light railway and a new pier in Sannox Bay were built. Of recent years the buildings have been considerably extended, and another shaft has been opened upon the hillside to the north. Over 10,000 tons have now been raised. Only the water power of the Sannox is used in the working of the mine. Barytes, when milled, is employed in the manufacture of paint, as a substitute for white lead.

Beyond Sannox Bay the road leaves the shore and runs inland up North Glen Sannox, thus cutting off the north-east corner of the island. Here in North Glen Sannox was once the largest village in Arran; but a hundred years ago, when the Highland clearances were in full swing, the whole of the families, to the number of five hundred persons, were transported to New Brunswick, where they formed a settlement at Chaleur Bay.

" Ah! wae's me ", lamented the Ettrick Shepherd, " I hear the Duke of Hamilton's cottars are a' gaun away, man and mither's son, frae the Isle o' Arran. Pity on us! was there a bonnier sight in the warld, than to sail by yon green shores on a brave summer's evening, and see the smoke risin' frae the puir bodies' bit shielings, ilk ane wi' its peatstack and its twa three auld donnered pines, or saughs, or elms, sugh-

sughin' ower the thack in the gloamin' breeze ". But these dwellings seem to have been primitive as well as picturesque, for Landsborough says that in North Sannox were " some of the poorest cottages I had ever seen inhabited by human beings ".

The road rises gradually to a height of 654 feet, and then descends by way of Glen Chalmadale to Lochranza. North Sannox is called a glen only by courtesy, for its sides spread outward rather than rise, and for most of the way we are walking over bleak exposed moorland. We see little of the mountains except the less interesting side of the north ridge of Glen Sannox proper, and the crown of the castles. Glen Chalmadale is more eventful, for the hills rise steeply on both sides to a height of a thousand feet.

By road the distance from Sannox to Lochranza is about seven miles. By following the coast the distance is increased to some ten or eleven miles, and, besides, the going is more arduous, for there is no road and not much of a path. About three miles from Sannox the Fallen Rocks are reached, where the end of a mountain ridge seems to have toppled over on the shore. Huge rocky masses strew the steep slope, like an avalanche rushing down to the sea.

The Cock of Arran, the northmost point of the island, is a large isolated mass of sandstone resting on the beach, a noted landmark among sailors. At one time this rock resembled a cock with wings extended in the act of crowing; but the piece which represented the head has long since been broken off. Somewhere hereabouts was born Daniel Macmillan, the founder of the publishing house bearing his name. A mile beyond the Cock is the Scriden (O.S. Scriodan), a headland strewn with immense masses of sandstone, more extensive than the Fallen Rocks but inferior to them in grandeur. Another mile brings us to Newton Point and the mouth of Loch Ranza. The houses of the village are scattered along the far shore, with the castle standing prominently before them.

Lochranza Castle, especially at high tide, is most picturesquely situated, for it is then surrounded on three sides by water. The stretches of mud that are exposed when the tide is out detract from the view. All that remains of the building is a roofless square tower with thick walls. It is mentioned as " a hunting-seat of the Scottish kings in 1380, when it was regarded as one of the royal castles;" but no part of the existing structure is earlier than the latter half of the sixteenth century.

In early times there was a chapel at Lochranza, situated on the east bank of the Balarie Burn as it emerges from Glen Chalmadale, of which nothing but a stone or two now remains. Although we have only records of a simple chapel, Scott in *The Lord of the Isles* locates the nunnery in which lived Edith, Maid of Lorn, upon this site.

Fishing is still carried on by a few of the natives; but the loch is no longer crowded with fishing-boats in the herring season. The summer visitor has been found to be less elusive and more profitable than the herring.

CHAPTER VII

Along the West Coast

The road still follows the coastline as we leave Lochranza, pass the pier, and set off on our way round the north-western shoulder of the island. To the north of us is Loch Fyne, to the west Kilbrannan Sound and the rough lonely coast of Kintyre. After little more than a mile of walking, as we enter the broad indentation of Catacol Bay, we pass the post office and the somewhat original row of houses which are known as "The Twelve Apostles". Half-way round the bay the burn issues into the sea from steep-sided Glen Catacol. At the entrance to the glen there are some fine terraces of alluvial matter. Here in Glen Catacol the white-tailed eagle continued to breed regularly until 1849. A pair nested there in 1870.

A battle is fabled to have been fought here between Fingal and his enemies, and a small mound, over the site of which the road now runs, was supposed to mark the spot where Fingal defeated the Norsemen under Manos, son of the king of Sweden. This is only one of the many legends told about Fingal and his son Ossian upon Arran. Fingal was born in the cave at Blackwaterfoot now known as the King's

Cave, and when quite a babe made a deep mark, two feet long, on the side of the cave with his foot. From this cave he used to step across to Kintyre and thence to Ireland by way of the Giant's Causeway. The standing stones upon Machrie Moor supported his pot while he boiled it. Ossian, it is said, traversed Arran repeatedly, on expeditions of love or war, on his way to Ireland, passing through the island on such occasions from Machrie to the *Cletes* at Clachaig (O.S. Clauchog) where he took ship. Ossian was married to the daughter of an Irish chief, and had a son by her whose name was Oscar. Oscar was killed in Ireland and his corpse was brought to Arran to be buried in Glenrie. Ossian had also a daughter or daughter-in-law, Malvina, resident at Drumadoon, whom he loved dearly. After Malvina's untimely death by accident or violence, her remains were burned and interred in an urn or pot under a cromlech at Drumadoon. On his last journey to Ireland, Ossian, now old and blind, got no farther than Clachaig, where he died and was buried: the cairn there marks his grave.

One cannot but admire the ingenuity of the Celt—his consummate lying if you wish—in explaining away prehistoric monuments by making them bear witness to the truth of his story. Mr. Hately Waddell, a " believer in authenticity by instinct ", who upon that principle would " rely on the authenticity of Ossian, whatever Dr. Johnson or his supporters might think or say to the contrary ", collected many legends and traditions about Fingal and Ossian in his ingenious but uncritical book on *Ossian and the Clyde.*

The green hill rises steeply to Meall nan Damh, nearly 2000 feet above us, as we leave Catacol Bay. About two miles from the Catacol Burn we pass a burial ground by the side of the road, one of the most desolate and neglected spots imaginable. Half a mile farther on, standing back a little from the shore, is the tiny settlement of Lennymore or North Thundergay. Between here and Mid Thundergay we cross the burn which issues from Coirein Lochain, by far the most picturesque of all the lochs of Arran. It is situated at the foot of the steep slopes of Meall Biorach, over a thousand feet above the sea. Ramsay, one of the earlier writers on Arran, described it in these terms: " The place is perfectly lonely—not a tree is near; and except the brown heath on its margin, and a few stunted rushes by the brook, the surrounding hills are almost bare of vegetation. The water is dark and deep, and the stormy blasts of the mountain never reach its still and unruffled surface. From its edge on all sides but that towards the sea, rise the naked hills, whose sides are formed of massive granite blocks, which, though surely yielding to decay, yet offer a stronger resistance to the destroying influences of time than the softer portions of the mountain, where the decomposing rock may almost be seen slowly crumbling away." It is curious to note that Landsborough, who quotes this passage, never actually saw Coirein Lochain, but commended it to other visitors on the strength of this description.

The Antlers of Dougrie

A mile from Mid Thundergay is Auchmore, or South Thundergay, with its clump of trees and, half a mile farther, Penrioch. Pirnmill, which we now reach, is bigger than any of these villages, being replete with boarding-houses and right on the shore. Almost continuous with Pirnmill but standing a little inland is Alltgobhlach. Then comes White-farland, then Imachar, then Balliekine, all with charms and partisans of their own. About eleven miles from Lochranza we reach Dougrie, at the mouth of the Iorsa Water, where we stop to regard the terraces in front of the shooting-lodge. These terraces are " the remains of a vast accumulation of detrital matter which once filled the whole of the deeply-embayed area at the mouth of the river, and was most probably deposited as a terminal moraine to two glaciers, which moulded the sides of Sail Chalmadale, and united their streams near the head of the bay." The shooting-lodge was built by one of the Dukes of Hamilton. The multitude of antlers that adorn the outside of the lodge walls is not a sign of heavy slaughter among the deer of the island, for the antlers are discarded by the deer each year, and can occasionally be found in the more remote inland parts. Those we see here were probably collected for the adornment of the lodge by shepherds and keepers.

We have now left the northern half of the island, and the ground upon our left, though still hilly, is no longer mountainous. Just before Machrie a road branches off inland to cross Machrie Moor and joins

The String about three miles farther on. We persist along the shore, with a stretch of golf links upon our left, until the road turns slightly inland as it approaches the Machrie Water. From Tormore it climbs gradually for a mile to a height of 178 feet. From its summit we have a distant panoramic view of the northern peaks. The road descending runs parallel for part of the way with the Black Water, through the largest and most fertile tract of arable land in Arran, till it reaches Blackwaterfoot, in Drumadoon Bay.

There is an attractive variation to the route we have just come. Leaving the main road at Tormore we make for the shore, and pick our way along the rocky coastline. After a mile we reach the opening of the King's Cave, one of the most interesting places on the island.

This cave, which is reputed to have been a favourite resort of Bruce and derives its name from that association, is formed out of firm white sandstone with a belt of red sandstone interposed. Its total length is over a hundred feet, its greatest width is forty-four feet, and its greatest height is nearly fifty feet. In January, 1909, when the soil upon the floor of the cave was partly excavated, the tusks of boars, the antlers of a deer, the bones of these animals, a block of refuse, and a small portion of a bronze ornament were found. But though the soil of the cave gave up only these trifling relics, its walls hold many interesting engravings—figures of horses and deer, concentric circles, a two-handed sword or a cross, a man with hands uplifted, a group of serpents, and two triangles with some sort of symbol within them. Unfortunately the original engravings have in several places been defaced or obliterated by the thoughtless cutting of names.

A seat has been cut out of the solid rock to the western side of the entrance, which has suffered greatly at the hands of selfish and thoughtless tourists. Bruce is said to have been seated here when a humble spider gave him that lesson in perseverance which inspired him to persist in the cause of his country's freedom. If there is any truth in this tradition the incident must have taken place while Bruce was on his way to Ireland, for when he returned he probably went straight from Rathlin Island to the east coast of Arran.

During the eighteenth century, meetings of the Kirk Session were frequently held in this cave, and during last century it was the school of the district for a considerable number of years.

There are several smaller caves, which were at one time distinguished as the king's kitchen, the king's cellar, and the king's stable. On the cliffs of the cave may be found, as a very appropriate adornment of a royal residence, *Osmunda regalis*, or the royal fern.

Leaving the caves we approach Drumadoon Point, where " high masses of stone lie in confusion at the base, then straight and clean rises for eighty or a hundred feet a façade of porphyritic columns, which are roofed with verdure ". Beyond the point we cross a mile of beach and golf links to reach Blackwaterfoot.

Arran was previously a stronghold of smuggling, "which, at one time, afforded a sort of occupation for a great number of young men", and illicit distilling. "The practice of illicit distillation," wrote the minister of Kilbride, in the *New Statistical Account*, "prevailed very generally not many years ago. But the heavy fines imposed of late on convicted delinquents, and the diminution of the gains of smuggling by the improvement of the spirits manufactured by the licensed distiller, have in a great measure put an end to this demoralizing traffic. Still the most upright of the common people are disposed to view it, if at all a breach of the Divine law, as at least a very venial one." The minister of Kilmory tells a similar tale. "Illicit distillation prevailed till a very recent period, but within the last ten years, very decided measures were taken for its suppression, and it is now almost entirely done away. Its demoralizing effects were not developed here so prominently, as in other places, from the circumstance of it being not considered a disreputable pursuit, and there being few, if any, in the parish, who, at some period of their lives, were not engaged in some department of smuggling. To the smuggler no stigma was attached on account of his employment; on the contrary, it was considered rather an honourable occupation, as exhibiting an intrepidity and art that acquired for their possessor a distinction in the minds of his companions. It was in the darkest night, and in the most tempestuous weather, when no cruiser would stand the gale, that, in his little skiff, the smuggler transported his cargo to the opposite shores of Ayrshire."

Smuggling has long since been given up; but illicit distilling went on for many years, and I have been told that till quite recently the curious visitor who swore secrecy could purchase in Blackwater-foot and elsewhere liquor upon which excise had not been paid. It was also said that those who did so were actuated rather by inquisitiveness or the desire to support local industry than by the love of the stuff, for it had a crude vile taste.

At Blackwaterfoot is one end of The String, by which we can cut across the island to Brodick. A mile and a half along it is the village of Shiskine. Here is to be seen a monumental effigy, found originally in Clachan churchyard, but now built into the wall on the west side of the chapel. It is the subject of an erudite article in *The Book of Arran.* Tradition has it that St. Molios is here represented, but there seems little doubt that the effigy is of a Cistercian abbot of Saddell, in Kintyre.

The String crosses the Black Water where it issues from Clauchan Glen upon the broad valley, passes Ballymichael and an odd farmhouse or so, joins the company of the Machrie Water, and then climbs gradually to a height of 768 feet. Approaching the summit we pass near one of the old forts, and a cairn which is said to mark the spot where St. Columba rested on his way across the island. At the highest point we pause to admire the panorama. To the north are the peaks—Ben Nuis, Ben Tarsuinn, the A'Chir Ridge, Ben Chliabhain, Goatfell, and the rest. Behind us to the west are the hills of Kintyre across the Kilbrannan Sound. Before us on the left is Glen Shurig and on the right Glen Cloy, running down to the wide expanse of Brodick Bay. To the south-east Holy Isle lifts its head above the intervening hills. To the south the hills of the plateau roll across the horizon.

Returning to the west coast to resume our circumambulation, we rejoin the coast about a mile from Blackwaterfoot. At the south end of Drumadoon Bay we pass the hamlet of Kilpatrick. Here was once in ancient times a chapel, possibly connected with the cashel of St. Brendan upon the hill above it. This chapel was so venerated in early times that bodies were brought from Ireland to be buried within its consecrated ground. This legend is corroborated by the fact that Arran is mentioned as a sacred burial place in *The Book of Kells.* Holy Isle enjoyed a similar reputation, and many bodies were taken from the east coast of Arran to Holy Isle for burial. Temporary burial was given until there were sufficient corpses for a shipment. The practice is said to have been discontinued after a ship containing bodies came to grief and sank in the Irish Channel. Part of the tradition was that the bodies were always carried over running water before being buried.

For two miles the road runs along the top of a

cliff, an inspiring place to walk when the wind is southerly. Below us the sea dashes upon the rocks, across the Sound Argyllshire comes to a stop in mid-ocean at the Mull of Kintyre, and away ahead of us we catch a glimpse in clear weather of the Antrim Coast.

The golf links interpose themselves between us and the coast as we approach Corriecravie and Sliddery. After the Sliddery Water is crossed we come upon the terminus of the other transinsular road. This road winds its lonely way up the valley of the Sliddery Water, past Burican—romantic name, Burican—under the shadow of Burican Hill, through Glen Scorrodale, over the summit at a height of 973 feet, where one is only a mere hundred feet below the peak of Holy Isle itself, down steep-sided Monamore Glen, and into Lamlash Bay.

About a mile from the juncture of the two roads is the dell, the most charming in the island, wherein lies the village of Lagg. Here, although only ten minutes' walk from the sea, one can enjoy the seclusion and tranquillity of an inland retreat. The inn—" as beautiful and picturesque as any Alpine hospice "—has been praised by travellers for a century at least, and I may add from personal experience that its traditions for hospitality are being worthily maintained. This would be an excellent holiday place for those who are not attracted by the mountains, especially in the earlier summer months. Later in the year one's temper and complexion are apt to be spoiled by midges.

CHAPTER VIII

Lagg to Brodick

The road leaves Lagg to run for several miles due east, at some distance from the sea. Alternately one can work laboriously along the shore past Bennan Head and the Struey Rocks, and rejoin the road near Levencorroch. The coast line is very broken, as numerous intrusive dykes run out to sea.

Levencorroch is a small village standing back a little above the road. About a mile later the road splits into two, one branch going up to the left, the other downhill to the right. The left inland road is the shorter, and passes Columbkille, one of several places on the island bearing the name of St. Columba. The road to the right leads us back to the shore again, where we are in full view of Pladda with its lighthouse, only a mile away. Rocky reefs run out towards it, and at low tide it scarcely seems to deserve the name of island. Away in the distance is Ailsa Craig.

These parts have seen several encounters between smugglers and revenue officers. Here between Pladda and Kildonan the king's cutter *Prince Augustus Frederick* ran down a salt smuggler. The smugglers and excisemen came to blows, which did not cease until one of the smugglers had been shot dead. Again, on 27th March, 1817, some whisky smugglers making for Ayrshire from these parts were intercepted by the revenue cutter, and turned and ran for the shore. Hastily beaching the smack they jumped ashore and, with the precious kegs on their backs, tried to escape. Thus burdened, however, they were soon overtaken by the officers, who took possession of the whisky and started to carry it back to the cutter. The inhabitants of the nearby cottages, witnesses of the chase and the capture, now took a hand. The officer in charge, John Jeffrey, appealed to them to keep clear or take the consequences; but the native blood was up and a struggle ensued. Jeffrey ordered his men to fire, which they did, killing two men of the name of McKinnon, and one woman, Isabel Nichol. Jeffrey was put on trial and was found " not guilty ".

Another Arran man, McKirdy by name, might have supplied Samuel Smiles with an example of success from most unlikely beginnings. While smuggling he met in with a revenue sloop, engaged it in combat, and came off victorious. A reward of £500 was offered for his capture. McKirdy turned up in person and claimed the reward. In some perplexity the authorities neither rewarded nor executed him, but shipped him off in a frigate as a bluejacket. He rose rapidly in the ranks, and in time was given the command of a frigate man-o'-war He played a lively part in the war with the French, but his career was brought to a sudden end one day when the crew of a French warship he had captured fired the magazine, and blew themselves and their captors to bits.

McKirdy's nephew also joined the navy, and worked before the mast until he became boatswain. One night, when lying off Boulogne, he was sent to reconnoitre. Seeing a French frigate with no sign of anyone on guard, he and his men boarded her, overcame the watch, battened down the crew below, and sailed her away. For this exploit McKirdy was promoted, and in time, like his uncle, was given command of a frigate.

As we pass through the scattered village of Kildonan we catch sight of its ruined old castle on the edge of the cliff overlooking the sea. Of the parts that remain, the ground floor has walls six feet thick, and the first and second floors have walls four feet six inches thick. Nothing seems to be known about this castle, except that it was built at some date between A.D. 1300 and 1500. The remains of a chapel have also been found in the neighbourhood.

We climb past the golf course to rejoin the other road, which leads us towards Dippin. Here we leave the road to explore Dippin Head, a range of precipices 300 feet high, rising sheer, over which a burn throws itself in a whirl of spray. These rocks form a counterpart, though on a small scale, to the great basaltic façades of Mull and the Antrim coast. "There is nothing on this part of the coast that equals in interest a pavement of basalt which extends from the sea line to the base of the cliffs. This causeway forms the nearest approach we have anywhere seen to the basaltic pavements of Staffa and the Giant's Causeway." Upon the summit of the Dippin Head is a shooting-lodge.

From Dippin the road runs northward for a mile and a half past Largymore and the Giant's Grave before Whiting Bay is reached. At the south end of Whiting Bay we cross the Glenashdale Burn, which calls for exploration. For a mile or so each bank of the river is well wooded. About a mile and a half from the road we come into sight of the highest waterfall in the island, bearing the name of Eais-a-Chranaig, where the stream descends more than 200 feet in two leaps. To the right of the waterfall, almost concealed among the trees, are the remains of an ancient fort.

Whiting Bay is rather a scattered town, as the houses of which it is composed are dotted along the road facing the shore, and over the hill that rises behind. Here are to be seen some of the most up-to-date buildings on the island.

At the north end of Whiting Bay, at Knockenkelly, the road and the shore part company once more. By following the path along the shore we reach Kings Cross Point, with its fort and Viking grave. The road, which has nothing of equal interest to offer, brings us in three miles to the meeting with the road across the island issuing from Monamore Glen, and shortly after we enter the outskirts of

Lamlash. From here we view the thin line of houses of all sizes spreading round the bay, with the Clauchland Hills rising behind. Out in the bay, in the shelter of Holy Isle, is an assembly of yachts, launches, and motor cruisers, and several large cargo boats, once employed in trade with India, but now brought here for cheap anchorage. At one time, when Lamlash was a naval base, the ships of the North Sea fleet used to foregather here.

Towards the south end of Lamlash, just where the road approaches the shore, and not far from the tennis courts, is Whitehouse. This was once the residence of Mr. Paterson, factor to the Duke of Hamilton, and a great improver of the surrounding country. "The rising grounds on each side yielded, some twenty years ago, a scanty crop of grass and heather; an extensive plain behind the house, if I remember aright, was full of peat holes; the ground before the house was a quagmire, on which the hungry cattle at times ventured, at the risk of being swallowed up. The quagmire has been converted into a beautiful verdant lawn; the undulating heights and the peat-producing plain are now waving with the richest crops, the house is embowered in flowering shrubs; and the garden is stocked, not only with culinary esculents and common fruits, but it yields also peaches, and nectarines, and figs." (Landsborough.)

It was from Lamlash, on the 25th April, 1829, that twelve families of Arran folk, who had been dispossessed of their land as a result of enclosure, sailed for Canada in the brig *Caledonia*. They were joined later by four Arran families who had come out in the ship *Albion*, and settled in Megantic County, some fifty miles south of Quebec. In an excellent work by a descendant of one of the Sannox emigrants, we are able to follow the fortunes of the exiles in their new home. This is *Annals of Megantic County, Quebec*, by Dugald McKenzie McKillop (Lyn. Mass., 1902).

The road runs right round the bay to within half a mile of its northern extremity, Clauchlands Point. From the end of the road a track leads up the hill to Clauchlands Farm. Just off Clauchlands Point the Hamilton Rock, the haunt of sea birds, rises above the waves. (This would appear to be the only memorial, among the place-names of Arran, of the powerful Hamilton family, who owned the island for so many centuries.) A steep cliff facing the sea stretches to the north-west of Clauchlands Point. About a mile from the Point, at a height of 536 feet, was once a fort, of which very little now remains. From the point it is possible, though not easy, to follow the coastline round to Brodick.

The more usual way of getting from Lamlash to Brodick is by the road leading off to the left a little beyond the pier. Less than a mile from Lamlash, across the golf course, and at no great distance from the road, is the ruin of the ancient chapel of St. Bride or Bridget. The building belongs probably to the fourteenth century, and is the only pre-Reformation church now remaining on the island.

A number of sculptured stones have been found near this structure, including one which has been thought to mark the grave of James, third Earl of Arran, who died in 1609 and was buried in Arran.

The Lamlash to Brodick road rises to a height of 375 feet. From its summit the peaks of Ben Nuis, Ben Chliabhain, and Goatfell seem to beckon to us from no great distance, sending forth an invitation and a challenge. From this Pisgah-view we descend by the road that winds through the wooded glen and brings us out at Brodick pier.

Holy Isle should be included in any thorough exploration of Arran. It can be reached in several ways—by the excursions which are occasionally run from Whiting Bay and Lamlash, or by hiring a boat at Kings Cross and rowing over.

Geologically the island is formed of an intrusive sill, imposed upon red sandstone which can still be seen, especially near the south at low tide.

The summit, Mullach Mor, is 1030 feet high, and can be reached by scrambling over heath-clad slopes from either the north or south end. Upon the east and west the hill descends very steeply, thus giving the island a more imposing appearance when seen from the shore or from out at sea.

The most important site on the island is St. Molios's Cave, on the western side, which was excavated in 1908 and is now in a fairly complete state, almost as occupied by the saint. A number of steps lead down into the cave, which is thirty-eight and a half feet long by thirteen feet at the widest part, and is partly paved with stone. Below the paving stones a drain had been cut out of the solid rock. At the south-west end, during the work of excavation, quantities of shells, bones, kitchen refuse, and a fireplace were brought to light. It is therefore presumed that the south-west portion was used for domestic and the north-east for devotional purposes. Runic inscriptions made by Norsemen, crosses from the hands of pilgrims, and initials cut by modern visitors are to be seen upon the walls of the cave.

Of the runes one has been made out to read, *Vigleikr the stallari cut.* The word *stallari* means Marshall, and as Vigleikr was Marshall to King Hakon, he probably cut the inscription in September, 1263, when the Norwegian fleet was in Lamlash Bay. There are others which read *Nikulos of Haene cut*, and *Sveinn*, and *Quondr cut the runes*, and *Amundre.* These may all be contemporary with that of Vigleikr; but there is another, *Olafr*, which is two hundred years older.

Not far from the cave is an almost circular sandstone block, with a level top and four seats cut in the sides. At the south side steps lead up to the top, and at the north end there is a hand grip on the upper edge and a step lower down. The diameter of the top is seven feet, the circumference of the middle thirty-one feet, and the height at the highest point seven feet. On the east side a curious cross with a ring top is cut, and some pilgrim crosses have been deciphered. This stone has been called both "St. Molios's Table" and the "Judgment Stone". The latter name probably gives us a clue to its function. Ecclesiastics sometimes acted as judges in early times, and the claimant may have stood at this stone while he stated his case. A roughly chiselled stone upon the lower side of the Judgment Stone was in all probability a receptacle for "holy water". A few feet away from the Judgment Stone is St. Molios's Well, which for centuries bore a surpassing repute among the superstitious for curing all sorts of diseases.

About a mile away from the cave, near the north-west corner of the island, is the reputed site of the monastery that once stood upon Holy Isle. In searching for traces of it a circular foundation was laid bare, which has been identified with the fortress built on Holy Isle by Somerled in the twelfth century. Some of the earlier monasteries were built of wood, and this may account for the fact that no definite monastic remains have been found. The monastery may have been responsible for the beginning of cultivation upon Holy Isle, as the site which is attributed to it is almost the only spot where anything could be grown.

Between this site and St. Molios's Cave is another cave, known as "The Smugglers' Cave". This cave was also used for ecclesiastical purposes, and a number of crosses cut upon the walls have been observed.

There are two lighthouses on Holy Isle, one opposite Kings Cross Point marking the passage into Lamlash Bay from the south, the other about half a mile distant upon the eastern coast. This latter beacon can be seen from Corrie.

CHAPTER IX

Rambling and Scrambling

One of the most common features of the Scottish landscape, the notice *Trespassers will be Prosecuted*, is lacking in Arran, and the visitor is allowed to wander almost at will. He is not compelled to admire the island's beauties and grandeurs from afar, but can explore the secret recesses of her heart, and lose himself in the innermost sanctuaries of her soul.

For myself, I have known few keener pleasures than those afforded by a day in the hills. To lose all contact with the petty restrictions of civilization, to strip and bathe in a swift clear pool of ice-cold water, to live for hours unseen by the critical eyes of others, is a refreshing and strengthening experience. Once or twice, as I lay with the sun beating down upon me, looking out over the broad expanse of the Firth, or halted, panting for breath, upon the steep side of Glen Sannox and surveyed the wide valley, I have become suddenly aware that I was no longer the citizen of a certain town, or a clerk in a certain office, but a part of creation itself, along with the sea below and the sky above and the rocks all round me. And even when the uplands are covered with a dimming, chilling mist, or the rain lashes down in biting blinding sheets, there is still the rougher sport of defying the elements, and taking delight in temporary discomforts.

A favourite ramble among visitors is from Brodick to Sannox by way of Glen Rosa and Glen Sannox. Bryce informs us that up to the year 1822 this route was known as practicable only by shepherds, some of whom occasionally used it. "But in that year two enterprising young ladies, Miss Alison and Miss Crooks, both from near Kilmarnock, but residing at Brodick, having arrived on a summer afternoon at the top of the ridge by passing up Glen Rosa, determined to try the descent into Glen Sannox, and return by the coast road. With great difficulty and loss of time they made good the descent; but were so late on arriving at Brodick that all the young men of the village had started off in parties, in different directions, to search for them. Their tale excited no little wonder."

From Brodick we enter Glen Rosa by following The String for a very short distance, then taking the road to the right just at the edge of a clump of trees. This road winds and bends and dips and rises, passes some white-washed cottages and a farm-yard, skirts the edge of a plantation, then, beyond the deer fence, degenerates into a mere track, and finally loses itself among the heath and bracken. Opposite to us, on the other side of Glen Shant, as this part was once called, rise the steep sides of Glenshant Hill, the southern extremity of the Goatfell *massif*. About a mile after we pass the deer fence we cross by a bridge over the burn called Garbh Allt, which comes down from the corrie (Coire a' Bhradain) between Ben Nuis and Ben Chliabhain.

The sides of the glen become loftier and steeper and rockier as we proceed northwards. On our left is Ben Chliabhain, rising grimly 2000 feet above us. Looking to the right our glance soars upwards over the bare grey flanks of Goatfell towards its summit. Ahead of us the lonely peak of Cir Mhor is now in sight. At our feet the Glenrosa Water winds its way between low heather-covered banks.

The head of Glen Rosa, where the five streams of the Glenrosa Water join one with another, is a wild bleak part hemmed in upon every side except the way we have come, by the mountains that surround it—Ben Chliabhain, the precipices of Coire Daingean, the A'Chir Ridge running northwards towards Cir Mhor, the Saddle, the north peak of Goatfell, the Stacach, and Goatfell itself. Lord Cockburn, who visited Glen Rosa in 1842, considered it "a valley worth passing a day in. All gushing with the clearest water tumbling over granite; deep sides, browned with chocolate-coloured autumn ferns, many dark rocky peaks, and the upper end enclosed by as striking an assemblage of black and picturesque precipitous mountain tops as is often to be seen." But surely his lordship meant *rarely* rather than *often*.

The Saddle, joining the peak of Cir Mhor with the *massif* of Goatfell, is the lowest point of this almost complete circle, although it is well over a thousand feet high, and thence we must make our way. The ascent is gradual, and the top of the ridge is broad and fairly even. From here we have our first glimpse into Glen Sannox. Steeply below us is the bottom of the glen. To our left Cir Mhor seems to rise from earth to sky in a single precipice. A semicircular ridge joins Cir Mhor with the crown of Caisteal Abhail, and from there the northern ridge of the glen runs out towards the sea. The skyline is broken by the V-shaped gap of Ceum na Caillich or Carlin's Leap, and the broad summit of Suidhe Fhearghas.

There are several ways of making the descent into Glen Sannox, which can generally be detected by the scratches of boot nails upon the rocks; but the easiest way is probably by a gully filled with earth and stone on the western side, close to Cir Mhor.

The floor of Glen Sannox is very wet at all seasons of the year, and to walk the length of it with dry feet is quite an accomplishment. The wisest method is to descend to the burn, cross it by the huge slabs some 150 yards past a big granite block with moss and heather on its summit, then keep to the path on its left bank until the workings of the barytes mine come into sight. The road is reached by the path leading past the mine and the graveyard. This glen is in the full-blown style, the grand manner: Macculloch described it as " the sublime in magnitude, simplicity, obscurity, and silence ".

Rambles from Brodick and Corrie

From Brodick excursions can also be made up Glen Cloy and Glen Ormidale or Gleann Dubh beyond to the summit of Cnoc Dubh (1341 feet), from which The String can easily be reached. The ridge between Ormidale and Dubh, Sgiath Bhan, offers some fairly mild scrambles over rocks. Coire a' Bhradain can be reached either by ascending Glen Rosa and then following the Garbh Allt until we reach the marshy floor of the corrie, or by striking north of The String at its highest point.

From Corrie or Sannox a visit should be made, even by such as have no intention of climbing, to the Devil's Punchbowl, for those who see it from afar have no true conception of its magnitude. Going farther afield, an excursion might be made to Lochranza by following the Sannox from its mouth to its source, scrambling up over the slippery wet slabs at the head of Glen Sannox, and crossing the low ridge connecting Cir Mhor with the Castles. Descending upon the other side, we traverse a landscape more gradual in its outlines until we reach the Iorsa Water. This we follow to its source, the pool Loch na Davie. From the other end of the pool flows another burn through Glen Easan Biorach, which we follow, waist deep in bracken most of the way, until we reach Lochranza. It is just as well to know the hours at which buses leave Lochranza for Corrie before starting this ramble.

The visitor to Lochranza can reverse this route, following Glen Easan Biorach up to Loch na Davie, then striking across for the ridge between the summits of Cir Mhor and Caisteal Abhail. From Loch na Davie one can turn in the other direction, skirt the sides of Ben Bhreac, descend into Glen Diomhan, and proceed thence back to the coast by way of Glen Catacol. Besides the path round the coast from Lochranza to Corrie the hills in the north-east corner call for exploration. This can be done in a day's walking by starting from the road between Lochranza and the Cock Farm at its highest point and keeping to the crest of the ridge running south-east for some four miles. We may then either descend upon the shore side at Fallen Rocks, or keep straight on for the village of Sannox, or follow a burn which leads us past the site of the fort into north Glen Sannox, where we rejoin the road.

Another upland walk which may be made from Lochranza or from any of the villages in the north-west of the island, is along the line of high rounded hills stretching from Glen Catacol down towards the mouth of the Iorsa Water. From the north the first summit, Meall nan Damh, can be ascended either directly from the road or from the rear by following Glen Catacol for a mile and a half before beginning to climb. From here we make southwards, first descending some 500 feet and then climbing again to the rocky ridge which forms the high ridge round Coircin Lochain. If we follow this semicircle round to its other extremity we should reach its highest point, Meall Biorach. The next summit, the highest of the three Ben Bhreacs, is less than a mile away, but more than 500 feet above us. From its topmost point we look down upon the desolate Loch Tanna, and across to the unsmooth outline of the eastern peaks. Tanna is rich in trout.

From Ben Bhreac we skirt round the head of the burn marked Glas Choirein on the map, and ascend Ben Bharrain, which is 2368 feet, the highest on this side of the island. From its summit we may see not only the peaks of Arran, but also the waters of the Atlantic, the Paps of Jura, and the mountains of Mull and Dalmally, and a long stretch of the Irish coast, from the mouth of Loch Swilly to the Mourne Mountains. To the south of Ben Bharrain is another summit only a few feet lower than it in height. From it we may either strike for the shore at Whitefarland, or continue southwards for several miles until we reach the Iorsa Water. In either direction the descent is steep at first and then becomes more gradual.

From Dougrie one might ascend the solitary hill called Sail Chalmadale, or traverse the interior of the island by following the Iorsa Water to its source and then descending upon Lochranza by way of Glen Easan Biorach, or explore the course of the Auchencar Burn and the hills that surround it. In general the southern half of the island does not offer the same variety of exercise and interest; but in suitable weather a bracing day can be spent tramping over the high moorland.

Three orders are to be distinguished among mountain worshippers: ramblers, or pedestrians, who go everywhere on foot and in an upright position; scramblers, who take delight in using their hands to surmount the lower stretches of rock; and rock climbers, who with heavily nailed boots and an Alpine rope attack the mountain upon its steepest side, and win to the top by dint of nerve and skill and perseverance. A wit once classified them as wenders, ascenders, and suspenders. I have just described the principal rambles, and shall now outline some interesting scrambles. Rock-climbing deserves a chapter to itself.

Most visitors to Brodick make the ascent of Goatfell. The path, which runs through part of the castle grounds, is plainly marked by finger-posts in its lower parts and higher up by small stone cairns. This path climbs the shoulder which runs out from Goatfell towards the sea, and then ascends steeply past the buttress of "boiler-plating" towards the summit. From Corrie the shortest way to get up is by following the White Water for some distance, and then cutting across and scrambling up over the rocks at the end of the shoulder. The summit is soon reached from there by the path.

One April day some years ago I climbed up this way alone. I started early, before the sun's rays had pierced the chilly mantle of night. The day promised fair, for scarcely a cloud was in the sky; but the fiercest wind was blowing that I ever encountered. As I walked along the road it whirled the tiny pebbles off the surface of the road and dashed them against my knees. Out at sea it whipped the tops from the high waves and scattered them like heavy rain. Up on the hillside, where the White Water splashed over the rocks, it blew the spray this way and that. I pushed on, enjoying the exhilaration of a new experience, until I reached the shoulder. Here the wind blew fiercer than ever. It rushed past my ears with a noise like an express train. Its gusts struck me in the face with the force of a blow. I had to lean against it to remain on my feet. I could scarcely breath or see where I was going. At last, when I was about the 2000 foot contour line, I decided to give it up, for although there was no danger of it blowing the twelve stone of me away it made my footing most uncertain.

From the summit of Goatfell on a clear day we look out upon a panorama as varied and extensive in its range, and as fascinating and impressive in its details, as anyone could wish to behold. To the east and north-east the Firth of Clyde is spread out like a geography lesson. There is the Ayrshire coast, running down to the Rhinns of Galloway and up towards the opening of Loch Long. There are the Cumbraes and the island of Bute. The small island off the west coast of Bute is Inchmarnock, also called " the Drunk Man's Island ", because offenders against the laws of sobriety in Bute used to be sent there to serve their term of punishment. To the north of Inchmarnock are the Kyles of Bute and Loch Fyne. To the west of us, across the abyss of Glen Rosa, the rocky ridge of Ben Chliabhain ends in the sheer sides of Coire Daingean, which is joined to Cir Mhor by the flying buttress of A'Chir.

Beyond, like the stump of a molar, is the top of Caisteal Abhail and the north ridge of Glen Sannox. Rising above Ben Chliabhain are Ben Nuis and Ben Tarsuinn.

"On a clear day, with a north-east wind, the panorama of the northern mountains is very fine. On the north-east horizon, Ben Lomond is easily known by its advanced position, elongated form, and double top—west of it on either side may be seen Ben Vorlich (Loch Earn), Ben Ledi, and perhaps Ben Lawers; north of it is the group of Loch Voil and Loch Dochart, among which Ben More is conspicuous by its conical form. To the north-west of Ben Lomond is the Arrochar group, among which Ben Vorlich, the Cobbler, and Ben Ime are the most conspicuous, the last, farthest to the north-west, of an elongated form like Ben Lomond, but higher, and with two tops. Still farther round to the north-west is the lofty group of Tyndrum, and Breadalbane forest, among which, perhaps, Ben Lui may be recognized, with a deep corrie on its south-east side filled with snow till far on in the summer. The wide extent of open undulating country, without mountains, between Loch Fyne and the sound of Kerrera, and bounded north by Loch Etive, renders it easy to identify Ben Cruachan on the east side, with its double summit, and Ben More in Mull on the west. Ben Nevis is less easily found; but having seen Goatfell from it on a very favourable day, we are quite sure it can be seen from Goatfell. It lies due north, far out on the horizon, and a little to the west of Ben Cruachan. The high group north-east of Mull is that which lies between Connel Ferry and Strontian; north of this are three conical mountains belonging to the district west of the 'Great Glen of Scotland', somewhere near Loch Lochy. Carrying the eye southward, we see the south promontories of Mull, with some low-lying isles, perhaps Staffa or Coll, across the north end of Jura, whose three paps are conspicuous and close at hand. South of Jura is Islay, well seen across Kintyre, whose two dependent islands, Davaar at the mouth of Campbeltown Harbour, and Sanda off the Mull, are under our feet. Across the top of Ben Nuis is seen Rathlin Island, south of which rises the lofty ridge of Antrim, of which the most conspicuous summits are Knocklayde, Aura, and Trostan, nearly 2000 feet in height; in the centre of Antrim Slemish is remarkable by its isolated position, and its form, a truncated cone. The bold promontories of the north coast come out in succession towards the west, Bengore, Macgilligan, and Malin Head; the top of the chain of Londonderry bounds the view in that direction. Far out southwards the eye may sometimes penetrate as far as the Isle of Man, and the groups of Morne and Skiddaw. In that direction, twenty miles south of where we stand, the grand cone of Ailsa rises abruptly from the sea; beyond, the eye ranges far out south-east and south, along the noble sweep of the Ayr and Wigtown coasts. As the day verges on towards evening, a purple curtain slowly falls over the scene to the south and east, while the light is still strong on all the northern mountains. Towards the west the islands stand grandly up in a sea of molten gold, which, rising far out westwards, blends with masses of gorgeous clouds 'set on fire with redness'—later still—

> The sun, descending
> Leaves upon the level water
> One long track and trail of splendour."

This description by Bryce is incapable of improvement. The modern wayfarer has the advantage of an indicator to assist him in identifying the prominent features of the landscape.

Having reached the summit of Goatfell an interesting "circular tour" can be made by following the ridge called the Stacach which runs north towards North Goatfell. (Perhaps I should call this ridge an *arête*, for whenever he passes the thousand-foot contour line the mountaineer takes on another language. A ridge becomes an *arête*, a furrow or crevice becomes a *couloir*, a sharp peak becomes an *aiguille*, a pass becomes a *col*, and a slide becomes a *glissade*. Also he ceases to climb or surmount or clamber over rocks: he "negotiates" them. If I seek to avoid these terms I trust my mountaineering friends will believe that I do so not from ignorance, but out of respect for the resources of our language.)

To resume our rocky way, the pass along the Stacach is fairly well defined. None of the turrets (or *gendarmes*, should I say) that stand in our path need balk us, for an active person can take them all in his stride with no great effort. The usual places of ascending and descending are clearly scratched on the rocks. At the farther extremity of this ridge we reach a high point to which the name of North Goatfell is commonly given. From it we have an exceptional view down into Glen Sannox. We keep to the ridge which forms the side of Glen Sannox, and make towards the mouth of the glen. The ridge becomes narrower and narrower, until we are walking along a mere comb which descends very steeply to the Devil's Punchbowl on the one side, and to Glen Sannox on the other. The name of Cioch na h-Oighe is given to this hill. The path along it is well defined, and there is no danger to anyone with a steady head. At the end of the ridge there is a steep though harmless descent through heath and over rock, and then a trudge over uneven uplands before the road is reached at Sannox.

An excellent " circular tour " of the ridge round Glen Sannox can be made by starting at Sannox and going back over the way we have just come as far as North Goatfell. From there we descend to the Saddle. Looking towards Cir Mhor from here we see one or two clefts running from top to bottom of the steep side facing us, where intrusive dykes have worn away quicker than the granite. We take either of these, and scramble over the loose stones and earth with which it is partly filled until we reach the top. We are now on the high shoulder of Cir Mhor. To reach the summit, we must skirt round to the left and approach it from the west.

The Ridge Around Glen Sannox

Having rested at the summit we take to the ridge round the very head of the glen, which brings us to the Castles, or Caisteal Abhail, the second highest point in Arran. The summit is extensive, and its formation is confusing, since four ridges run out from it. The most important is the one dividing the north and south Sannox glens. By following it for three-quarters of a mile we reach that far-seen landmark, Ceum na Caillich, or the Carlin's Leap. The descent into it is very easy; but the other side is a great tower of granite boulders some 150 feet high, and its ascent belongs to the section on rock-climbing. It can be avoided by descending about thirty feet on the north Sannox side and then traversing round ledges of mixed rock and turf, and approaching the summit from the east. From here to Suidhe Fhearghas, which is a bump rather than a peak, is about a mile, and thence we descend either into Glen Sannox or to the road in north Glen Sannox.

Another semicircle of high ridges can be climbed by ascending Ben Chliabhain from Glen Rosa, scrambling northwards to Coire Daingean, then crossing by way of Beallach an Fhir-bhogha or the Bowmen's Pass to Ben Tarsuinn and back by way of Ben Nuis. This is really a good day's work.

The only scramble in the west of the island is along a ridge running in a north-westerly direction from Ben Bharrain. It is half a mile long, fairly narrow, and falls steeply on both sides. Hands have often to be used, but a rope is not necessary.

CHAPTER X

Rock-climbing in Arran

Of late years there has been a healthy increase in the number of climbers that go to Arran, and ropes and boots are seen much more commonly than before among the luggage that is unshipped at Brodick. This is an encouraging sign, for the mountains have more to offer than strenuous exercise. The perfect mountaineer has the fingers of a gymnast and the arms of a wrestler, the endurance of an athlete, and the courage of a hero, the balance of a dancer and the nerve of a steeple-jack, the eye of an artist, and the perception of a mystic. No such person ever existed; but only by making this our ideal and striving towards it, shall we fit ourselves for the company of the mountains.

To the mountaineering beginner I would give this advice: get a strong, well-nailed pair of climbing boots, not too big, and an old pair of plus-fours, and practise on the slightest provocation. (Better climbers than either of us have kept in training by hanging from kitchen stairs, and climbing on to mantelpieces.) Seek the company and advice of more experienced climbing friends remorselessly. And do not neglect to acquire such information as is imparted in books like *First Steps to Climbing* by Abraham, *British Mountaineering* by Benson, *Mountaineering Art* by Raeburn, and the general introduction to mountaineering published by the Scottish Mountaineering Club.

Arran has both advantages and disadvantages as a training ground for the climber. It offers a large number of climbs all generally accessible from one or two centres, and these climbs differ greatly in the difficulties which they present. The climber, also, is usually rewarded for his labours by a fine view from the summit. On the other hand all the considerable climbs are on granite, and there is little variety in the nature of the rock between one part and another. Climbing on weathered granite makes one suspicious and wary. In a measure this is a virtue, but it cramps one's style, and leads one in Skye and the Lake District to mistrust footholds and handholds which are perfectly safe.

Though the peaks are commonly covered with snow in winter, the snow is not deep enough, and the frost is not keen enough to justify the use of ice-axe, crampons, or skis. We must go to the mainland, above all to the Cairngorms, to enjoy the full rigours of winter mountaineering.

Now if the Arran peaks were in England they would have been mapped out long ago, and the climbs described, and each handhold and foothold detailed, in a dozen books. As it is we have to seek guidance from the excellent but not universally

The Boulders and A'Chir Ridge

accessible *Journal of the Scottish Mountaineering Club.* Volume X of that *Journal* contains an expert and exhaustive climbing guide to the island of Arran by H. MacRobert.

Let us begin with those fine trial places, the boulders along the shore. About 400 yards to the north of Corrie schoolhouse, on the shore side of the road, is a large boulder, properly called Clach an Fhionn or the Hero's Stone, but commonly known as the Elephant Rock. At its side is a smaller boulder. The best climb is up between the two, and so by a small crack to the summit. The climb from the rear is easier. Clach Mhor (the Great Rock), to the south of the White Water, can be ascended by only one route, three sides being inaccessible. Clach a' Chait or the Cat Stone is the most difficult of the boulders. The climb on the west side is probably the easiest. There are two routes from the side towards the road; the one to the left calls for considerable muscular effort, and the other has never been accomplished without a " shove-off ". The steep Rocking Stone can be climbed from the road by those with strong fingers.

The most delightful climb in Arran is the traverse of the A'Chir ridge, which is rightly marked " for mountaineers only " by Benson in his fine book on *British Mountaineering*, yet is not really so dangerous as either Cioch na h-Oighe or Cir Mhor. This ridge forms the face of the recumbent figure which was once called " Lord Brougham in his Nightcap ", but which now, when Lord Brougham and nightcaps are alike forgotten, goes by the name of "The Sleeping Warrior". From Brodick the best route to the south end of the ridge is by Glen Rosa and Coire Daingean, which lies across the glen from the summit of Goatfell. Having reached the top of the ridge we keep to it as long as possible. Upon the Iorsa side it descends steeply, and the Rosa side is a "continued precipice". There are two gaps in this comb where it is impossible to keep to the actual ridge. The first of these, that is, the one farthest from Cir Mhor, is generally tackled by descending on the Iorsa side, the other by descending on the Rosa side. This brings us up to the side of Cir Mhor. The sharp shoulder running out from Cir Mhor towards Glen Rosa, the Rosa Pinnacle as it is sometimes called, has afforded some strenuous sport and interesting practice.

The tors which rise from the summit of the Castles offer good climbing. The difficult eastern side of the Carlin's Leap is climbed in this manner: Ascend the easy chimney which starts a few feet above the ground, and runs diagonally upwards for ten feet or so. At the top of this chimney is an earth landing, from which the climber has to surmount fifteen feet of a smooth-sloping granite slab. This is the most difficult part of the climb, and the beginner may require either a pull from above or a push from below. There follows fifteen feet of smooth grass, a rock wall ten feet high, another fifty feet of steep grass, then (to the right, between two huge masses of rock) a chimney fifteen feet high leading towards the summit. When he has come so far without assistance, and then scales the boulder that crowns the summit, the climber has accomplished one of the trial pieces of the island, and is no longer a novice.

From the floor of the Devil's Punchbowl the side of Cioch na h-Oighe rises about 800 feet at a general angle of 60°. Crossing this face, rising from left to right, there are five well-defined ledges, chiefly of heather and grass. These ledges are denoted by the numbers 1 to 5, 1 being the outermost and 5 the innermost. All can be ascended; but this is no place for the tyro, and the fate of a youth in the Punchbowl some years ago illustrates the dangers of solitary climbing. A shallow gully, which runs perpendicularly down the face of Cioch na h-Oighe crosses the lower three of these ledges, and the place of crossing is in each case rather difficult to pass, for the ledge disappears and the climber has to step from one foothold to another with nothing much to detain him, if he slips, until he reaches the bottom of the cliff, some hundreds of feet below. I must admit that, although I have climbed this cliff several times, I have an aversion to such "bare-faced" work.

The chief difficulty in ledge Number One lies about a third of the way from the top, where the ledge dwindles away to almost nothing for about fifty feet. Number Two is quite easy, except at its lower end, which is very steep. The lower sixty or eighty feet of Number Three are very narrow, but as most of the footholds are on sound rock the difficulty is not great. The upper parts are broad and easy, except where they are crossed by the perpendicular gully. Number Four is not well defined for the lower 100 feet, and a traverse has to be made over a steep rock-face sprinkled with tufts of heather, and without many good holds. Higher up the footing improves, though the ledge is very narrow for another 100 feet or so. Number Five consists of heather and grass throughout, and forms a perfectly easy and simple route to the top. It is, however, narrower and longer than some of the others, and there is one somewhat sensational corner to go round. The following is the order of difficulty: Two, Five, Three, One, Four. Probably the best climb on Cioch na h-Oighe was that accomplished in June, 1896, by Messrs. Haskett-Smith and Naismith, who climbed up " smooth and not very steep rocks, from near the foot of Number Three ledge, and struck ledge Four fully a third of its height up ". Leaving Number Four higher up, a " short climb on some good rocks " brought them out near the summit.

The precipitous face of Cir Mhor which looks down upon Glen Sannox is typical of the kind that repels the pedestrian and attracts the mountaineer. At first glance it appears impossible; but in 1894 a regular siege was instituted, and several routes were discovered and explored. They are described in an article on Cir Mhor by Gilbert Thomson in Volume III of the *S.M.C. Journal*, from which the accom-

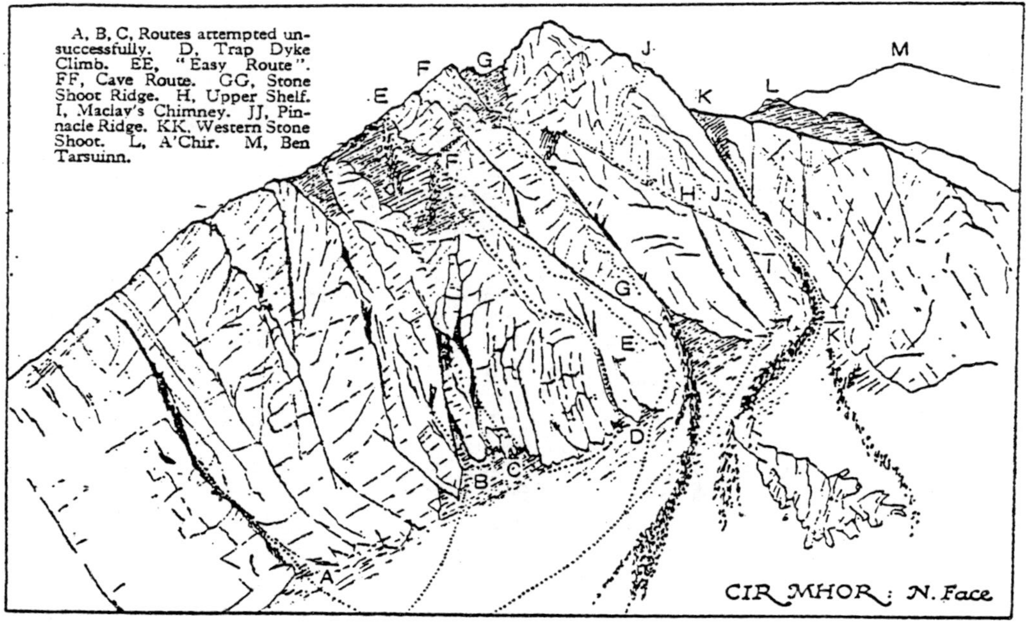

CIR MHOR: N. Face

A, B, C, Routes attempted unsuccessfully. D, Trap Dyke Climb. EE, "Easy Route". FF, Cave Route. GG, Stone Shoot Ridge. H, Upper Shelf. I, Maclay's Chimney. JJ, Pinnacle Ridge. KK, Western Stone Shoot. L, A'Chir. M, Ben Tarsuinn.

panying illustration is taken by permission. D marks a gully which must be ascended over wet and crumbling rocks, discomfort being the chief difficulty. This leads up to a grass patch, from which the route FF can be followed—one of the most interesting stretches on the whole face. A narrow gully leads up from the grass, and ends abruptly in a cave, the roof being formed of enormous wedged blocks. The passage through the top of the cave was found rather narrow by the first climbers, and called for much wriggling; but it is now much wider, thanks to the efforts of those that have passed that way. The top of the cave has a small cairn, marked by Δ on the line FF. The grass patch can also be reached by the variation starting at E. The easiest way up the face of Cir Mhor would be to follow the grass to the ridge—that is, from E to E. The lower part is rock scrambling of an easy kind.

The route marked GG is known as " the stone shoot ridge ". It has been climbed several times. A small cairn has been marked by a Δ. The upper shelf H was attacked in the hope of finding a way to the top; but it ended abruptly. The north-west pinnacle ridge JJ offers a fine climb, and in addition a way has been found to reach the shelf round the ridge. The western stone shoot, KK, is a mere walk except in one place where a steep rock face has to be avoided by climbing out of the shoot.

These are still the main routes up the Cir Mhor face; but subsequently variations have been discovered and recorded. A very difficult ascent has since been made, for example, by B route by a gully which joins route EE. The intrepid veterans, Raeburn and Inglis Clarke, were the first to follow this route. (See *S.M.C. Journal*, vol. V, p. 29.) I cannot say whether it has ever been repeated.

Ben Chliabhain, Coire Daingean, the Bowmen's Pass, and Ben Tarsuinn all offer attractions and problems to the climber, and there are doubtless a few places in which " first ascents " can still be made. Little serious interest seems to have been paid to the steep Glen Rosa side of Goatfell.

The most sensational climb on Arran was the ascent of the Ben Nuis chimney by Baker, Puttrell, and Oppenheimer in 1901. It is described by Baker in his book *The Highlands with Rope and Rucksack*, and Oppenheimer wrote an account of it which appeared in the *S.M.C. Journal* in January, 1902.

The chimney or deep fissure which was climbed runs from top to bottom of the crags of Ben Nuis a little south of the peak. Even from Brodick, more than four miles away, the thin black line is visible. When observed more closely, the chimney is seen to alter its angle about half-way up. To the right of the peak is another gully, well-marked but not so prominent, which was first climbed by Green and Boyd in 1895, by following the gully for some distance and then making an upward traverse to the left until they reached the summit. Inglis Clark and Raeburn also ascended the two easy gullies to the left, and tried the lower slabs of the chimney, which they pronounced impossible.

The foot of the chimney seemed simple, for it consisted of a rounded slab which did not appear very steep. It was in three sections, first an easy fifteen feet, with a grass ledge on top, then twenty feet rather steeper, then another fifteen feet slab. Both the middle and the third stretch proved more difficult than they looked, and were very wet. As Puttrell, from Oppenheimer's shoulders, swarmed up, the stream of water ran through his clothes, and bubbled out at his boots. In the next pitch the gully became narrower, and cut deeply into the mountain. Forty-five feet above them was a group of jammed stones. Puttrell surmounted this by "chimneying" up, with his feet against one wall and his back against the other. There followed another stretch resembling the water-slide but much steeper, which was conquered at the third attack. They were now in a deep and narrow cleft, with an inclined floor so slippery that they had to wedge their backs and their feet against opposite walls to maintain their position. Above them, 170 feet up, massy fragments had blocked up the chimney completely. Puttrell swarmed up to it, and finding it impossible to attack directly he climbed to a ledge outside the chimney. To do this he had to turn round, and at the same time keep himself in position by bracing against the sides—a very difficult feat. The others had at least the moral support of the rope in following him.

In order to regain the chimney above the jammed stones, Baker, the lightest of the party, stood upon Puttrell's shoulders, pulled himself up towards "a flimsy coating of grass and bilberry", and then made a precarious traverse upwards and back until directly over the others. "The footing was bad, nothing but a yielding cushion of turf and bilberry; but it was wasting time to search for a rock ledge." From this position he assisted them to ascend with the rope. Another forty feet of chimney which were fairly easy, a stretch of broken rocks, and fifteen feet of stiff back and knee work brought them to a deep grassy platform, with a new problem set well at the back of it. This was a fifty feet chimney, divided throughout its length by a thin rib. Both divisions looked feasible, but the granite was so smooth in one place, so rotten in another, that nothing could be done. At this point they had been climbing for six hours, and had only done 240 feet out of the 400.

Baker then offered to try the steep tufts of grass on the left wall. As he cautiously climbed from one to the other, Puttrell and Oppenheimer stood well back in the recess, prepared, in case of a slip, to pull him in on to the grass platform. "It was smooth and ledgeless except at the joints, where tufts of herbage sprouted, and here and there where the decayed rock left a crumbling corner sticking out that might lend a little support if handled gingerly. . . . With the hand disengaged I undid the rope, pulled it up, and tied myself on again at the end. Forty feet higher, and seventy above my companions in adversity, I found a safe stance, from which a plain and easy course appeared right to the summit."

In this ascent so much depended on the strength of grass and herbs—"vegetable holds", as the mountaineer calls them in his contempt—that it would be foolhardy for anyone to attempt to repeat it. There are sufficient climbs which call for skill and strength and nerve, without relying so heavily upon Providence and good luck. Yet these three deserve the praise due to those who carry a daring venture through to a safe conclusion, and one of them at least tasted the joy of achievement.

"The sun set as we went down. Not only the forky pinnacles of Arran, but also the peaks of the mainland as far north as Ben Cruachan stood out against a sky of immaculate purity. Eastwards the cloudy outline of the Ayrshire hills marked, as it were, the boundaries of night. The encircling sea had the unearthly tints of evening; Ailsa Craig was a soft shadow floating on deep blues and violets; the stony crests all about us gleamed and flushed. What were physical discomforts and fatigue with such glories around us?" (Baker, *op. cit.*)

CHAPTER XI

Animal Life

Britain was joined to the continent of Europe until a period that was, speaking in terms of geological history, quite recent. By the land bridge between what is now France and England many of the animals of Europe crossed into Britain, and became the ancestors of the animals that still live there. Not all of the European animals found their way thither, a fact which can be demonstrated clearly by the results of an animal census. While Germany has about ninety species of land mammals, Britain has only forty, and while Britain has only thirteen species of reptiles and amphibia, her nearest continental neighbour has twenty-two.

A kind of Wallace's Line should also be drawn round Arran, for there are several species common on the mainland and the neighbouring islands—the mole, the stoat, the weasel, the squirrel, and probably the fox and the wild-cat—which do not occur on Arran. The hedgehog is of rare occurrence, and the rat, the mouse, the hare, and the rabbit owe their presence there to the agency of man. It seems reasonable to conclude that Arran was separated from Scotland before Britain was separated from Europe. Several of these species are also missing from the Orkneys and Shetlands.

The red deer is undoubtedly the most picturesque and the most interesting of the animals that now inhabit Arran. The roe deer has been extinct for many years.

"The highest Hills of this Island," wrote Martin two centuries ago, "are seen from several parts of the Continent and *North-west* Isles, and they serve instead of a forest to maintain the deer, which are about four hundred in number, and they are carefully kept by a forester—to give sport to the Duke of *Hamilton*, or any of his family, that go hunting there. For, if any of the natives happen to kill a deer without license, which is not often granted, he is liable to a fine of £20 *Scots* * for each deer. And when they grow too numerous, the forester grants licenses for killing a certain number of them, on condition they bring the skins to himself."

After a time they became scarcer, and Pennant records that in 1772 "the stags, which used to abound, are now reduced to about a dozen". The original breed was never exterminated, and in 1859 fresh blood was imported from the mainland, which had very salutary effects upon the herd. In 1872 there was estimated to be about five hundred of them upon the island, and at present they probably fall little short of that number.

I suppose most of us have watched from above

* The pound Scots was equal to 1*s*. 8*d*. sterling.

a line of hinds with their young threading their way up Glen Rosa, leaping burns with effortless grace; or espied a moving patch of reddish brown among the green grass away up on the other side of Glen Sannox; or been regarded by a herd of stags whose antlers were spread against the sky like the tracery of a Gothic window.

A full-grown red deer stag stands about four feet high at the shoulders; the hind is somewhat smaller. Their summer coat is short, glossy, and reddish-brown; but in winter it changes to brownish-grey, and becomes long and rough. The under parts are light, and there is a white patch round the short tail. The young are spotted until the spring after their birth. The stags and hinds live apart for the greater part of the year, the stags generally choosing the higher ground. Towards the end of September comes the mating season, when the hills resound with the roaring of stags as

"The wild buck bells from the ferny brake."

Savage combats take place between rivals, and the conqueror wins several wives. The young are calved in May or June, and are kept hidden in the bracken or at the side of a wood.

The antlers of the stag fall off in March and are replaced before August each year. Their growth is said to keep pace with the growth of the bracken among which he rests. Discarded antlers, sometimes bearing teeth marks where the stags have chewed them, are occasionally discovered in secluded spots.

On Deer and Antlers

Antlers are usually regarded as weapons; but they are not the only means of attack and defence, as stags often fight very effectively with their teeth and hoofs.

In books on the red deer, which are sometimes not without a melancholy chapter on the cooking of venison, one comes across a wealth of obscure terms relating to the deer and their antlers. " When the male Deer-calf is a few months old he becomes distinct from the female by the appearance of two knobs (' bossets ') on the front of the head; he is then a *knobber*. Next year these become large and pointed (' dags ') and he becomes known as a *brocket*. The third year a branch appears forward—the brow antler—and he becomes a *spayad*. The fourth year a second forward antler—the bez-time or bay—is produced at about a third from the summit of the now long horn, and he is known as a *staggard*. The tray (très) or royal antler appears near the summit in the fifth year, and this entitles the young deer to the title of *stag*; he has come of age. From the sixth year, when the crown of antlers begins to form at the summit by the production of tines in several directions at the same height, he becomes a *Hart* or *Stag of Ten;* and in former days he could advance beyond that dignity by escaping with his life after being hunted by the King, thereby earning the rank of a Stag Royal." (Step, *Animal Life of the British Isles.*) Twenty years would seem to be a good age for a stag: hinds probably live much longer.

Other Mammalia

Although we associate them with mountains and moorlands, red deer are originally woodland animals. They feed for the most part upon grass and heather tops; but prefer the leaves and shoots of trees. One of their most popular feeding-places in Arran is a clump of bare trees, about 500 feet above sea-level, between Corrie and the Devil's Punchbowl. They are very fond of cabbages, carrots, potatoes, turnips, and corn, and do great damage wherever they are allowed entry, hence the high dykes and fences that are seen in many parts of north Arran. They frequently come down to the shore to eat seaweed. Late one evening I surprised half a dozen stags among the rocks near the White Water, and with my torch sent them scampering up the hill at an amazing speed.

In Arran the red deer are kept down by discriminate shooting. Towards autumn one sees a warning flag raised upon the ridge of Cioch na h-Oighe, and a few fine stags, dead and gralloched, lying near the roadside, waiting to be taken to the Castle. But for the most part they are not molested, and one can approach within sight (though rarely within focus) of them without much trouble.

The other mammals indigenous to Arran are the common bat, the long-eared bat, the common shrew, the black water-shrew, the otter, the brown rat, and the common field-vole. Wild goats, which once inhabited the heights of Arran, are now extinct there; but may still be seen upon Holy Isle.

The Adder

Another animal met with in Arran is the adder or viper. Occasionally its not ungraceful shape is seen rising above the grass, or wriggling to cover over the stones; but in general it avoids detection, and has to be sought out by those who wish to view it.

The average adder is less than two feet in length, though the female of the species quite commonly exceeds that by a few inches. A wide variety of colouring is found, especially between the two sexes; " but, generally speaking, it may be said to be some tint of brown, blue, or grey, and this ground colouring may be so dark that the darker markings are scarcely perceptible on a cursory view. Along the sides there are whitish spots, sometimes reduced to mere dots. The brown, red-brown, or olive males have black markings; the grey or whitish males are marked with brown or black, and have the underside black. The throat is black, or whitish with scales spotted or edged with white. The females if brown or brick-red have dark-brown or red markings; olive females have brick-red bands or spots. The yellowish-white chin and throat are sometimes tinged with red." (Step, *op. cit.*)

For the most part the adder spends the summer upon sandy heaths, dry moors, and the sunny slopes of the hillside or wood, and feeds upon mice, shrews, voles, and other small mammals. In autumn it retires to the dry moss or the discarded ground-nest of a bird, and remains there till April.

Most of us must admit a feeling of revulsion at the sight of an adder, or indeed any form of snake;

but this is an attitude which we should try to overcome, and even if we cannot, we should never allow it to lead us to seek the creature's destruction.

The adder shuns the company of man, and cases of adder bites are rare in this country. I don't suppose anyone has been bitten by an adder in Arran for years, although many of us wander barelegged up hill and down dale. And even when it does occur the bite of an adder is no very serious matter to a healthy adult: unpleasant results can generally be avoided by sucking the wound and applying oil to it.

In numbers adders have long been on the decrease in Arran. Pennant says of Holy Isle that "the walk is far from agreeable, as the island is greatly infested with vipers". And Landsborough tells us that on the way from Brodick to Corrie "a person does not require to leave the road to find what might be more rare than pleasant, viz. poisonous adders, which come out of the wood to bask in the sun. These, I think, have been reduced in number since Brodick became so much frequented; for, some years ago, a person could seldom pass along this road on a fine day without seeing an adder, either dead or alive." Coming nearer to our own day Bryce says, "The adder (*Pelias berus*) is often met with in the glen, on the dry parts of the path, and in places where there is a dry bottom under the heather; and the tourist in crossing these will do well to use caution. Again and again we have narrowly escaped treading upon them in such situations here, on the North Sannox shore, in Lamlash Glen, and other places. We have never seen them higher, however, than the top of Glenshant Rock, 1100 feet; nor are they as abundant on the west as on the east side of the island, on account, no doubt, of the shelter and warmth." Nowadays one can go anywhere on the island without giving them a thought.

The seas around Arran also abound in life, from the mighty whale to the microscopic plankton. Whales are quite frequently seen in the Kilbrannan Sound. Most of them would appear to belong to the family of Bottlenose whales, one of which was captured in Loch Ranza in 1883. Porpoises fish round the coast at all seasons of the year. Seals, though not exactly a familiar sight upon the Arran shore, are never far away, and can usually be seen on the lonely rocky shore of the Little Cumbrae. Paddling round in my canoe I have often surprised them as they lay basking. One inquisitive seal followed us for miles up Loch Fyne.

Practically every summer accounts appear in the newspapers of fishing parties attracting a shark, and having a narrow escape from it by rowing like fury for the shore. There are, admittedly, dozens and dozens of sharks in the waters around Arran, especially in Kilbrannan Sound and the mouth of Loch Fyne, in the spring and winter; but there is little reason to fear them, as they are practically all basking sharks, and quite harmless. The basking shark is the largest in the North Atlantic, and grows to a length of forty feet and more: one twenty-four feet long was stranded at Bennan Head on the 30th August, 1922, and I have seen three, which looked no smaller than this, sporting together about a quarter of a mile outside Holy Isle.

The basking shark is not predatory, and feeds on the small floating organisms in which the seas abound. Even if molested or attacked it offers little resistance. At one time it was hunted in the same manner as whales, as its liver yields a valuable oil. The name of Basking Shark is derived from its habit of remaining motionless at the surface. It is also called the Sailor, because the two fins by which it is readily recognized stand up like sails.

Many attractions await the entomologist in Arran, for "gorgeous and swift-flying Red Admirals, Fritillaries, and Painted Ladies are common among the butterflies, and vicing with them in speed and beauty are the great Emperor and Oak Eggar moths. The Convolvulus Hawk moth, which measures some five inches across, has also been taken here."

The smaller creatures that inhabit the shores of the island and the seas that surround them form an interesting branch of study, as all who have read Dr. Newbigin's fine book on *Life by the Seashore* are prepared to believe; but this is not the place to discuss them at length. Lists of the different mollusca, crustacea, echinodermata, and so on are given by Landsborough, by Bryce, and in the British Association *Handbook*.

CHAPTER XII

The Birds of Arran

Few places in Britain offer opportunities for observing bird life so conveniently or so extensively as Arran, for there one finds both an abundance of the commoner and also a few of the rarer species, which elsewhere have become extinct. For myself, I should never dream of going tramping without a book in my pocket to assist or verify the identification of less common birds. I usually carry *A Bird Book for the Pocket*, by Saunders; but there are others which may be quite as good. Besides the information to be found in this and similar books of reference, there are clever sympathetic studies of many of the birds to be found in Arran in *Wanderings of a Naturalist* and other works by Seton Gordon.

Among off-shore birds the star performer is the gannet. Most visitors must have admired it as it suddenly plunges from a height of a hundred feet or more into the sea below. During this plunge it keeps its prey in sight, as it can sometimes be seen to swerve, or even check its dive, up to the last instant. A Dunure fisherman has captured a gannet in his nets at a depth of ninety feet, and there are doubtful reports of Ballantrae fishermen having taken them in the nets at twice that depth. This bird, which is seldom seen over land, breeds upon Ailsa Craig, and flies as far afield as Ireland, France, and Portugal.

The Great Northern Diver, also unworthily called the Loon, is common till late in the spring, and is often caught in the nets. It is one of the handsomest of sea birds: its upper surface is a chequered pattern of black and white, the under parts are white, and the throat is streaked with black and white. Its dive is a rapid somersault, it makes a quick turn and disappears head first, tail last. Its true home is farther north, in Iceland and Greenland. The smaller Red-throated Diver is more familiar, and at one time bred on the shores of Arran. It is about the size of a wild duck. Its throat is a rich chestnut, and the neck grey, with vertical lines of black and white.

The Stormy Petrel, that dainty little bird, is sooty black in colour with a little white about the tail and under the wings, and in size is no larger than the orchard chaffinch. It keeps to the open sea except when nesting, and is frequently seen between Arran and Ayrshire. It may breed on the Clyde as in the Hebrides, but its nest is very hard to find. When breeding the birds only emerge after sunset, and feed their young and make their flights by night.

The Cormorant and the Shag are familiar sights along the shores of Arran, though they do not breed upon any part of the island. Both are large black birds with a metallic sheen of green. When alarmed they swim half-submerged, with their long necks sticking out of the water like periscopes. For a few months in spring the Cormorant has a conspicuous white spot upon the thigh, by which it can be distinguished from the Shag when in flight. It is besides, a bigger and heavier bird than the Shag. The Cormorant is frequently seen on inland waters, the Shag only on the sea.

Of the duck tribe the Tufted Duck, the Golden-Eye, and occasionally the Scaup and the Pochard are seen off-shore in winter diving for food. The Mallard and the Teal are common at all times of the year, and when a wild duck is mentioned it is usually one of these two which is implied. They keep closer inshore, and paddle about instead of swimming and diving. The Sheld-duck and Red-breasted Merganser are also residents, but are much less numerous than the Mallard and the Teal. The Wigeon is another winter visitor.

The Golden-Eye is distinguished by the dazzling white of part of the plumage against the adjacent black or brown: even at a distance one can see a large white spot at the base of the bill of the full-grown drake. The Scaup, like the Tufted Duck and the Golden-Eye, has a conspicuous white bar on its wings. The foreparts of the mature drake are glossy black, the flanks and underparts white. The duck is brown and chocolate, with grey breast and white stomach, and is by no means easily distinguished from the female of the Tufted Duck or Golden-Eye.

The Mallard is the most common freshwater duck in Britain, and is familiar to all in its domestic state. The tame duck differs from the Mallard only in its heavier body and shorter wings. The Teal is the smallest and most approachable of the duck family. It has a patch of glossy green round each eye, the rest of the head being chestnut. Its upper parts are grey, with a good deal of black and white and green showing.

The Sheld-duck is boldly marked in black, white, and chestnut, which has led one observer to speak of its finely harlequin appearance. It is only doubtfully a member of the duck family, for it has several affinities with geese.

The Wigeon is midway in size between the Teal and the Mallard. Its large white wing-patch is as conspicuous in flight as on the water. The drake has also a light patch upon its forehead, hence the name occasionally given to it of Baldpate.

The Red-breasted Merganser is easily distinguished by its red eye and bill, its glossy green head and crest, and its white collar. The under parts are white. It forms a link between the diving ducks, like the Golden-Eye, and the Divers, for it varies fish-fare with the crabs, small molluscs, and other food to be found on the shore. It dives like a Cormorant, and has also that bird's ability to swim half-submerged.

The lanky desolate figure of the Heron, the picture of resignation, haunts the quiet rocky parts of the shore. An old saying had it that when the

Herons left the island the Dukes of Hamilton would go too; but the dukes are gone, and the Herons still remain. Popular legends notwithstanding, the White Stork is a very rare visitor.

"The largest gull with the black mantle is the Great Black-backed Gull. The medium-sized gull with the black mantle is the Lesser Black-backed Gull. It is distinguished from the larger species by its smaller size, and by having yellow legs and feet, while the legs and feet of the other are flesh-coloured. The Herring Gull, which is roughly the same size as the Lesser Black-backed Gull, has a pale-grey mantle. Of the three smaller species, the Black-headed Gull can be recognized in summer by its dark-brown head. The head is nearly white in winter, but at all seasons of the year it can be recognized by its red bill and feet. The other two small gulls with the grey mantle are the Common Gull and the Kittiwake Gull. The Common Gull has green feet and bill, while the Kittiwake has black feet and a yellowish bill. On the extreme point of the wings the Common Gull has white, while the tips of the wings of the Kittiwake are almost completely black. These descriptions apply only to the adult birds. At all seasons of the year many gulls are to be seen with the whole plumage of different shades of dull grey and brown. These are immature birds of the different species. It takes several years for gulls to acquire the distinctive adult plumage." (McWilliam, *The Birds of the Island of Bute.*)

Of these six, the Lesser Black-backed Gull is

principally a summer visitor. The others are resident throughout the year, though only the Common Gull is known to breed. Occasionally the Arctic Skua is seen, a large dark gull that robs other birds of the fish they have secured.

The Tern, or Sea Swallow, is smaller and more graceful than the gulls. It dives, or rather pounces, upon its food from the air, and does not rest upon the surface of the water. It is a summer visitor, and is not so common around Arran as along the shores of Loch Fyne.

The Razorbill and the Black Guillemot are frequent visitors, and the Puffin, which until recently bred upon Ailsa Craig in great numbers, sometimes finds its way thither.

The Oyster-catcher is the most conspicuous of the birds that inhabit the shore, for its plumage is a contrast of intense black and pure white, while its legs are red, and its strong bill orange-yellow. The Oyster-catcher does not feed on oysters, but is an expert hand at mussels and limpets, and flies with a noisy scream from rock to rock in search of them. The Turnstone, which is a sort of second cousin to the Oyster-catcher, and with its party-coloured livery and orange legs, one of the most beautiful of the wading birds, visits Arran in winter. Its name is derived from its habit of tipping over flat stones for the sake of the sand-hoppers, worms, and other small fry which it finds beneath. Turnstones are also known to help each other turn over stones. Of the Oyster-catcher's other relatives the Ringed

Plover, the Golden Plover, the Lapwing or Pewit, the Dunlin, the Redshank, the Curlew, the Snipe, and the Woodcock are all residents, the Purple Sandpiper is a winter and the Common Sandpiper a summer visitor, the Whimbrel is a bird of passage, and the Curlew Sandpiper, the Greenshank, the Bar-tailed Godwit, and the Jack-snipe have occasionally been seen.

The Ringed Plover is a sociable bird, and even during the breeding season is commonly found in small parties. It has a conspicuous collar of white and black. Its upper parts are brown; but for the rest it is a pleasing mixture of black and white. It usually betrays its presence by sounding an alarm when approached. The name of the Golden Plover is an indication of its most prominent distinguishing mark, and its clear, wild, far-reaching call of *Tlu-ee* is often heard on the moors. The Lapwing is a familiar sight throughout Scotland, and for that reason its amazing grace and beauty is often overlooked. The Dunlin generally outnumbers all other members of the wading tribe. It is a small bird, from seven to eight inches long. In summer it is mottled chestnut and black above, and ashy grey with a touch of white below. In winter it is ash-grey above and white below. The noisy Redshank can be distinguished by its size (slightly greater than that of a Missel Thrush), by its long straight bill, and by its red stilts. It nods its long neck and beak up and down, like a disciple of St. Vitus rather than of St. Francis.

The Purple Sandpiper is dark hued with a purple glint, relieved by yellow legs and a white patch on the wings, conspicuous in flight. It is not very large, only eight inches in length. The Common Sandpiper is not so dark in plumage. The beak of the Curlew Sandpiper is curved downward. The Bar-tailed Godwit is a little larger than the Oyster-catcher, but stands much higher on its long stilts. In flight its head and neck are tucked in like a Heron's. Like a Heron, too, it stands dreaming upon one leg. It is distinguished from the Curlew (or Whaup) by its straight bill and by the streaking of its under parts.

Of the small song-birds the following are found in Arran: the Greenfinch, the Goldfinch, the Twite, the Lesser Redpoll (fairly common), the Linnet (common at all seasons, especially where there is gorse), the Bullfinch (not numerous), the Chaffinch, the House Sparrow (deplorably common), the Tree Sparrow, the Corn-bunting (becoming rarer), the Yellow Bunting (or Yellowhammer or "Scotch Canary"), the Reed Bunting (not uncommon), the Meadow Pipit (here, as elsewhere, the most frequent victim of the Cuckoo), the Tree Creeper, the Great Tit (common), the Coal Titmouse, the Long-tailed Titmouse (in small numbers), the Gold-crested Wren or Goldcrest (common though not conspicuous, usually frequenting the woods), the Stonechat (fairly common, but extremely local), the Robin, and the Wren.

Of the larger birds we have as residents the Missel

Thrush, the Song Thrush, the Blackbird, and the Starling. The last is, comparatively speaking, a newcomer. It only began to breed in Ayrshire a hundred years ago. Before that time it was practically unknown in Scotland except in the Orkney and Shetland Islands, and the Outer Hebrides. It is now one of the commonest species, in Arran as elsewhere, especially in the neighbourhood of human habitations. Skylarks occur both as residents and as birds of passage. Frequently they are observed at Pladda Lighthouse, where they sometimes rest on the parapet all night and then depart when morning comes.

By the river banks one often sees, at all times of the year, the Grey Wagtail and the Pied Wagtail. The White Wagtail, which is really drab rather than white, is a not uncommon visitor. Much rarer is the Yellow Wagtail, a bird of the meadows rather than of the stream. The Dipper, or Water-ouzel, is stout and compact in body and a little smaller than a song thrush in size, and has been aptly described as a big black wren with a silvery white bib. The Dipper is something of a curiosity, for though it is in no manner suited for such work, so far as we can see, it moves freely and feeds under water, in the pools of mountainous streams. The Moorhen or Coot may also be mentioned here.

Among trees the Wood Pigeon is a common nuisance, and the Stock Dove and the Ring Dove also exist. The owl family is well represented, for we have the Long-eared Owl, the Short-eared Owl, the Tawny Owl, and most beautiful of all, the White-breasted Owl.

Although Arran is by no means a bird sanctuary, yet it has, of recent years at least, been ruled wisely, and several birds of prey, which elsewhere have been hunted to extermination, are allowed to live unmolested. And even if the Kite and the White-tailed Eagle, the Hobby, and the Hen-harrier no longer live there, it is to be hoped that we shall always have with us the Peregrine Falcon, the Merlin, the Kestrel, the Sparrow Hawk, and the Golden Eagle.

The Peregrine Falcon, which is usually represented by about eight nests, is the noblest of the hawk family, both in its heraldic appearance, and in its indomitable courage. Whereas the eagle feeds for preference upon carrion, the Peregrine Falcon takes its prey in full flight, often striking down birds much heavier than itself, and very rarely failing to make a kill. This is the hawk most commonly used in falconry, and when James, Earl of Arran, sent to the island for hawks in 1505, it was doubtless these birds which were intended.

There is, as a rule, one nest of Merlins each year. The Kestrel, which can usually be identified by its hovering in the air, and the Sparrow Hawk are much more abundant. At one time Golden Eagles flourished in Arran, but a misguided Duke of Hamilton issued orders for their extermination. The last of them was kept chained up like a dog. " This descendant of the ancient cloud-cleavers of the isle has been a captive, we are informed, for about twenty-nine years, yet still he is lusty and well feathered, and retains a large portion of his native ferocity and courage. His principal food seems to be fish, but this we suppose is more from necessity than choice, as he lately made short work with a poor chicken which incautiously ventured within the scope of his tether." (Macdonald, *Days at the Coast*, 1860.) In recent years, however, the eagle has returned, and is now carefully protected.

The ravens usually build eight nests in Arran each year, and are frequently to be seen and heard in the Devil's Punchbowl. Generally one hesitates to give away the location of a bird's nest, lest the information be wrongly used; but the Raven is quite capable of building out of the reach of the egg-collector. The Hooded Crow and the Carrion Crow, that unpopular pair, both occur, and hybrids between the two, which resemble Rooks in appearance but are distinguished by their hoarse croak, are commonly seen. There used to be four Rookeries in Arran; but some years ago the Rooks were killed or driven away, and are now rarely seen. The Jackdaw still flourishes.

Among the birds of "sporting" interest are the Black Grouse, the Red Grouse, the Pheasant, and the Partridge.

The following are summer visitors to the island: the Tree Pipit (occasionally), the Spotted Flycatcher (in small numbers), the Chiffchaff, the Willow-warbler or Willow Wren (common), the Whitethroat (common), the Ring-ouzel, the Wheatear (regularly), the Whinchat (not uncommon), the Redstart, the Swallow (common), the House-martin (much less common), the Sand-martin (not numerous), the Swift (common), the Nightjar (common), the Cuckoo (frequently seen on the moors, usually accompanied by protesting Meadow Pipits), and the Corncrake (often heard but seldom seen).

The following table, adapted from *The Birds of the Island of Bute*, by Rev. J. M. McWilliam, gives the average date of first arrival in the Clyde area:

Lesser Black-backed Gull,	12th March.
Wheatear,	30th ,,
Sand-martin,	10th April.
Swallow,	10th ,,
Chiffchaff,	13th ,,
Common Sandpiper,	14th ,,
Willow-warbler,	15th ,,
Ring-ouzel,	20th ,,
Yellow Wagtail,	21st ,,
Cuckoo,	24th ,,
Tree Pipit,	25th ,,
Corncrake,	25th ,,
House-martin,	25th ,,
Redstart,	27th ,,
Whinchat,	29th ,,
Wood-warbler,	1st May.
Swift,	2nd ,,
Common Whitethroat,	3rd ,,
Sedge-warbler,	3rd ,,

The Brambling, the handsomest of the finches, the Fieldfare, and the Redwing are the chief winter visitors. Among the birds which have been occasionally seen, and for which the experienced bird-watcher should keep a keen look-out, are the Rose-coloured Starling, the Crossbill, the Snow Bunting, the Great Grey Shrike, the Dotterel, the Greenshank, and the Water Rail.

There remains the obituary, birds which once found a home in Arran and are no longer to be seen there. We have mentioned the Kite, the Hobby, the White-tailed Eagle, and the Hen-harrier. The Hen-harrier, to be sure, is still seen occasionally in winter, but no longer comes to Arran to breed, as it once did. The Magpie, the Jay, the Chough, and the Kingfisher appear to be extinct as breeding species. Here belongs also, apparently, the Quail, the Ptarmigan, and in spite of attempts to re-introduce it, the Capercailzie.

CHAPTER XIII

Flowers and Plants

The fourth edition of Bryce's *Geology of Arran* contains "an account of the Flora of Arran drawn up by the author's eldest son, Mr. James Bryce, now of Lincoln's Inn, and Regius Professor of Civil Law at Cambridge," better known as Viscount Bryce of Dechmont, statesman, traveller, and writer. One is naturally reluctant to leave such good company, consequently I have, by kind permission of Viscountess Bryce, borrowed this account of Arran's flowers and plants in large measure from him.

The richness of Arran as a botanical field is owing to two causes—its geographical position, being at once insular and near the mainland, and its physical structure, which gives rise to the greatest possible variety of situation and soil, from lofty and precipitous mountains, widespread moors, and small alluvial plains to hot and sheltered glens, damp woods, and sandy seashores. The mild climate with its copious rainfall is also an important factor. Everyone must have observed how much of the peculiar charm of Arran scenery is owing to this circumstance. The bright green of the fields and pastures, the woods that fringe the shore and cling to the slopes of the lower hills, add grace and soft beauty to landscapes that would otherwise be severe and gloomy in their grandeur; and while they pleasingly relieve the monotonous grey of the granite mountains, serve to heighten by contrast the effects of the bare crags and jagged peaks that rise behind them. In spring or early summer, when the grass sprouts fresh on the hillsides, and the varied foliage of the trees still preserves the delicate green of youth; or in July, when the lower ridges are purple with the rich heather-bloom, this variety of colour is finest —and this is the best time to see Arran scenery in its perfection. While, again, if we turn our attention from the general outlines of the scene, and look more closely at its details, we shall find no less cause to admire the effects of an atmosphere moist and warm. To it is owing not only the abundant growth of natural wood which clothes the glens and sea cliffs, but also the size and splendour of many of our finest shrubs and wild flowers, such as the laburnum, the hawthorn, the fox-glove, the honeysuckle, and perhaps most striking of all, the luxuriant profusion of the whole fern tribe from the stately *Osmunda* or Royal Fern to the lowly *Hymenophyllum* or Filmy Fern.

Most of its common species—the plants of the field, the roadside, the marsh—Arran has in common with the western lowlands of Scotland, and these lowland plants form the bulk of its Flora. They include most all those of common occurrence, as well as several of the rarer sort—such as *Ranunculus*

Lingua (Great Spearwort), *Helianthemum Chamæcistus* (Common Rock Rose), *Cephalanthera ensifolia* (Narrow-leaved Helleborine), *Samolus Valerandi* (Brookweed), the *Botrychium* (Moon-wort), and *Ophioglossum* (Adder's Tongue), *Asplenium Ruta-muraria* (Wall-rue Spleen-wort), &c. Under this class are embraced nearly all the species that frequent the cultivated land, the marshes and streams, the woods and pastures; together with several maritime ones—as *Silene maritima* (Sea Campion), *Œnanthe Lachenalii* (Parsley Dropwort), *Calystegia Soldanella*.

A second "type" discernible in Arran is that which we might call the Highland. To this group belongs the alpine plants of the highest granite mountains—*Salix herbacea* (Least-Willow), *Thalictrum alpinum* (Alpine Meadow-Rue), *Alchemilla alpina*, *Cryptogramme crispa*, and others; several also occurring in elevated situations in various parts of the island—as *Sedum roseum*, *Oxyria digyna*, *Hymenophyllum peltatum* (One-sided Filmy Fern); besides a few found in mountainous regions, though at no great altitude—such as *Corydalis claviculata* (White-climbing Corydalis), and *Phegopteris dryopteris* (Oak Fern).

There is, thirdly, in Arran a class peculiar to the west coast, and especially frequent in the Hebridean chain of islands. Such are many of the maritime species—*Brassica monensis* (Isle of Man Cabbage), *Sedum anglicum*, *Raphanus maritimus*, as well as *Pinguicula lusitanica*, *Gymnadenia conopsea* (Fragrant Orchis), *Drosera anglica*, and *Listera cordata* (Heart-leaved Tway-blade)—plants found in various localities through the interior. This class includes many of the most interesting and characteristic plants of the island—not a few of them such as will be entirely new to the English botanist.

But the most curious feature in the botanical geography of Arran is the occurrence in its southern extremity of several species scarcely to be found elsewhere in Scotland; belonging, in fact, to the flora of central England, and here apparently quite projected, so to speak, from their ordinary range. Of these the most remarkable are *Lathyrus sylvestris* (Everlasting Pea), *Verbascum Thapsus* (Great Mullein), and *Carlina vulgaris* (Carline Thistle). They all occur within the circuit of a mile, on the warm southern face of the cliffs and steep alluvial banks that front the sea at the extreme south of the island, near Bennan Head. No one who examines the locality can think it possible that they should have escaped from cultivation; and it is scarcely less improbable that they should have been planted there by the hand of man.

Most of the rare plants of Arran are to be obtained on or near the coast, some decking the bright sands, as the *Brassica monensis*, the purple *Mertensia*, or oyster plant, as it is called from the flavour of its leaves, and the lovely *Calystegia Soldanella*, with its creeping stems and flowers of delicate pink; some dwelling in the salt marsh and wet grounds that lie between the old sea cliff and the present tide mark, such as *Œnanthe Lachenalii*, *Triglochin maritimum*, and *T. palustre* (Arrow Grass), the pretty little *Glaux* (Sea Milkwort), the blue *Aster*, and several others. Here, too, though not properly maritime plants, we often find the handsome *Parnassia*, and delicate *Anagallis tenella* (Bog Pimpernel), *Samolus Valerandi*, *Orchis latifolia* (Marsh Orchis), and in the drier spots *Geranium pratense* (Blue Meadow Crane's Bill), *Erythræa littoralis Fries.* The bare rocky crags and promontories, which here and there diversify the generally accessible coast of the island, are gay with the brilliant white, yellow, and pink flowers of *Sedum anglicum* and *S. acre* (Biting Stone-crop), *Silene maritima*, and *Spergularia marginata* (Seaside Sandwort-Spurrey); the succulent *Cotyledon* (Pennywort) fixing its roots in the rock clefts, and the glossy green of the sea spleenwort, *Asplenium marinum.* The curious sea cliff which lines the coast of the island in almost every part, marking the level at which the sea stood in some former age, is in most places thickly covered with a natural growth of oak, ash, birch, hazel, and other trees, and is kept moist by the numerous streams that trickle down its face, or precipitate themselves in cascades from its edges. The shade and humidity thus produced render its vegetation luxuriant and varied; and we find many interesting species growing on or near this line of irregular cliff, some hanging from its wooded sides, some springing rank in the wet caves that pierce it, and some inhabiting the stony and marshy ground at its base.

Here, among others, occur *Veronica montana*

(Mountain Speedwell), *Hypericum Androsæmum* (Tutsan), *Geranium sanguineum* (Bloody Crane's Bill), *Sanicula europæa* (Wood Sanicle), *Eupatorium cannabinum* (Hemp Agrimony), *Lycopus europæus* (Gypsywort), *Listera ovata* (Tway-blade). Here, too, most of the Arran ferns may be found—*Phegopteris dryopteris* (Oak Fern), and *P. polypodioides* (Mountain Polypody), *Cystopteris fragilis* (Bladder Fern), *Polystichum aculeatum* (Prickly Shield Fern), *Asplenium marinum* (Sea Spleenwort), *Hymenophyllum tunbridgense* (Tunbridge Filmy Fern) and *H. peltatum* (One-sided Filmy Fern), and the magnificent *Osmunda regalis* (Royal Fern). I do not mean that all these plants are to be met with in any one spot, but that they all occur in some part or other of the sea cliff, while many abound through the whole of its long extent. Those species which have just been mentioned, with the addition of one or two rarities, such as *Cephalanthera ensifolia* and *Thalictrum flavum* (Common Meadow-rue), form in the main the sylvestral flora of the island, which it is therefore needless to speak of more particularly. Similarly, there is little to distinguish the vegetation of the lower glens from that which has been described as characteristic of the sea cliff and the woods, not, at least, till the point is reached where the larger trees grow scarce, finally giving place to thickets of birch or hazel, or to the open expanse of pasture and moor. Here the aspect of the scene changes, and plants quite different attract the attention of the botanist. The greensward is gay with the purple *Gymnadenia conopsea* (Fragrant Orchis), as beautiful as it is fragrant, the blue *Jasione montana* (Sheep's Bit), *Pimpinella Saxifraga* (Burnet Saxifrage), *Gentiana campestris* (Field Gentian), *Erythræa Centaurium* (Common Centaury), *Cœloglossum viride* (Frog Orchis), and *Leuchorchis albida*, *Orchis maculata* (Spotted Orchis), and many other handsome plants. Nestling among the heather we may find *Circæa alpina*, *Listera cordata*, with its slender stem and minute yellowish flowers, the taller *Galium boreale* (Cross-leaved Bed-straw), and the tender green of the oak fern, *Phegopteris dryopteris*. *Rubus saxatilis* (Stone Bramble) here and there trails its long stems over the stony ground, while the viscid leaves of the sundew *Drosera rotundifolia* and *D. anglica*, the tiny cream-coloured flowers of *Pinguicula lusitanica*, the straggling yellowish-green stems of the little *Lycopodium Selago* (Fir Club-moss), mix with the moss that grows thick round the margin of the springs and rivulets.

The moors in the south, varying in height from 900 to 1400 feet, have little to interest the botanist. He may travel over them for a whole day without meeting more than two or three species among the coarse grass and heather, mixed with rushes and cotton grass, which clothe the surface of the peat moss. Generally it may be said that the flora of the higher grounds in Arran is inferior to that of the low country. The granite mountains in the northern part of the island rise quite into the alpine region, and are often covered with snow. Yet when compared with the mountain tracts of the central highlands, they will be found to possess few alpine plants. The commonest plants on the high mountains are *Saxifraga stellaris* and *Alchemilla alpina;* the former is scarce on Goatfell, occurring more abundantly on the heights round the head of Glen Sannox; the latter is very frequent on all the high peaks, and covers, with the graceful drapery of its silky leaves, the ledges of many a granite precipice. *Salix herbacea*—the dwarf willow, whose woody stem scarcely rises from the ground—is found on most of the principal summits; *Circæa alpina* and *Saxifraga hypnoides* occur occasionally near the summits of the southern hills; the pretty little *Thalictrum alpinum* may be found in many places, as on Ben Bharrain, on Goatfell, at the head of Glen Cloy, and on the summit of the pass leading from Glen Rosa into Glen Sannox; *Cryptogramme crispa*, the parsley fern, has been noticed in several spots, rooting deep among the loose blocks of stone that strew the mountainside, while among the cryptogamous plants, *Phegopteris dryopteris* and *P. polypodioides*, *Crystopteris fragilis*, *Hymenophyllum peltatum*, and several of the alpine *Lycopodia*, may be enumerated as denizens of the glens and mountains.

Regarding the water plants of the island, those which we find in its marshes and streams, there is but little to be said. They are few in number, and not in any way remarkable. The list is nearly exhausted by the names of *Hypericum elodes*, *Ranunculus lingua*, *Drosera anglica*, *Littorella uniflora*

(Shore Weed), *Alisma plantago aquatica* (Water Plantain), and *A. ranunculoides* (Lesser Water Plantain), and several species of *Potamogeton* and *Carex*. Of true lake plants there are very few; and this fact suggests the remark, how deficient Arran is in picturesque lake scenery. Loch Tanna, by far the largest of the lochs, is set in a scene of utter wildness and desolation, without grandeur.

A few concluding words may not be amiss to direct the botanist to the districts where his rambles will be attended with most pleasure and success. Probably no part of the island will offer to him so many interesting species as the vicinity of Brodick, especially if he direct his walks to the Corriegills shore, proceed northwards to Corrie, or explore the tangled thickets and dripping rocks at the head of Glen Cloy. Around Loch Ranza, too, several excellent plants may be obtained; while, even if the tourist be not botanically inclined, he will find in the exceeding beauty of the coast an ample reward for his walk along the lovely shore between Glen Sannox and Newton Point. The western shore offers many striking scenes, and everywhere commands noble views of the broad sound of Kilbrannan, with Kintyre beyond; but its botany presents little that is new to one who has already examined the eastern part of the island; while the interior of the country is occupied by undulating granite mountains, seldom, except at Glen Catacol, assuming forms of sublimity or beauty, and clothed with no vegetation beyond the grass and heather that grow among the slowly decomposing blocks of grey granite with which the ground is strewed for miles. Such is the aspect of the country —bleak, wild, unvaried—from Loch Ranza to Loch Iorsa and Dougrie.

Despite what has been said of the botanical attractions of Brodick, there is no district in Arran which will better repay the trouble of a visit than the south coast, from Sliddery to Whiting Bay. Without any of the alpine grandeur of the north, it has many striking beauties of its own—smiling little bays, steep green banks, and bold cliffs of basaltic rock, porphyry, or claystone, jutting far out among the waves, or running in tall colonnades along the shore; seaward there is the wide expanse of glorious blue, with the magnificent pinnacle of Ailsa full in front; beyond all, closing the distant horizon, the gleaming cliffs of Ayrshire and the far-off coast of Ireland. It is a delightful shore to wander along slowly, searching and prying for rarities in the salt marsh by the water's brink.

The mountains at the head of Glen Sannox will be found richer in alpine plants than Goatfell, though inferior in height. Yet even their flora must appear scanty and uninteresting to one who has botanized over the ranges of the central and eastern Highlands, Ben Lawers, Braemar, or Clova. But at this he will have no cause to repine when he finds himself led into some of the most magnificent mountain scenery in Britain.

APPENDIX I

PLACE-NAMES OF ARRAN

In the following list the names, except where stated, are Gaelic. The Ordnance Survey gives these hints for pronouncing Gaelic.

Initial *Bh* or *Mh* equals *V*, but after a broad vowel equals *W*, as in English " now ".

Initial *C* equals *K*.

Initial *Fh* is silent.

Initial *Ph* equals *F*.

Initial *Sh* or *Th* equals *h* in " human ".

Initial *S* after *An t* is silent.

A'Chir, the comb crest.
Achag, a little field.
Allt an Eas, the glen of the waterfall.
Allt Goblach, the forked river.
Allt Tigh an t-Siorraim, the burn of the house of the sheriff.
Am Binnein, the little hill.
Arr Fhionn, Fingal's slaughter.
Auchencar, the field of the rocky land.
Auchencairn, the field of the cairn.
Auchengallon, the field of the standing stones.
Auchmore, the great field.

Ballarie, the house of the shieling.
Ballikine, the stony or steep lea ground.
Ballymichael, Michael's stead.
Beinn a' Chliabhain, the hill of the little cradle.
Ben Bharrain, the hill of the little gap.
Ben Bhiorach, the hill of the heifer.
Ben Bhreac, the dappled hill.
Ben Nuis, the hill of the fawns.
Ben Tarsuinn, the cross or transverse hill.

Place-Names

Benlister, the hill of the vessel.
Bennan, a little hill.
Blairbeg, the little field.
Blairmore, the great field.
Burican, a peat moss.

Caisteal Abhail, the forked castle, or the ptarmigan's castle.
Catacol (Norse), rift of the wild-cat.
Ceum na Caillich, the carlin's leap.
Cioch na h-Oighe, the maiden's breast.
Cir Mhor, the great crest.
Clachag, the stony place.
Clachan, a church and burying ground.
Clachland (a hybrid), stony land.
Clach Mhor, the great stone.
Cnocan, a little hill.
Cnocan Kelly (*Knockenkelly*), the little hill of wood.
Cnoc Dubh, the black hill.
Coillemore, the great wood.
Coire Daingean, the corrie of the fort.
Coirein Lochain, the corrie with the little loch.
Columbchille, Columba of the churches.
Corrie, a cauldron.
Corriecravie, the hollow of the trees.
Craw, a sheepfold.

Dippin, black pennyland.
Drumadoon, the ridge of the fort.
Dun Fionn, Fingal's fort.

Eas a' Chrannaig, the waterfall among the trees.

Garbh Allt, the rough burn.
Glaster, the blue water.
Glen Ashdale (Norse), the glen of the ash tree.
Glen Cloy, the stony glen.
Glen Dubh, the black glen.
Glen Kill (*Kiln*), the glen of the wood.
Glen Ree, the king's glen.
Glenscorrodale, the glen of the deep gully.
Glen Shant, the sacred glen.
Glen Shurig, the glen of the colts.
Gortonalister, Alexander's cornfield.

Place-Names

Imachar, the place of the ridges. (Arable land was once divided in ridges.)

Kil. " Originally this denoted only a hermit's cell, though it was afterwards used to mean the church of which the hermit's cell was so often the germ. They often point out to us the earliest local centres from which proceeded the evangelization of the half-savage Celts; they direct us to the hallowed spots where the first hermit missionaries established each his lonely cell, and thence spread around him the blessings of Christianity and civilization."—*Isaac Taylor.*

Kildonan, the cell of St. Donan, who flourished *circa* A.D. 560.

Kiscadale, the causeway of the vale.

Lagg, a hollow.

Lagan, a little hollow.

Largy Beg, Mor, Meadonach, the little, big, middle hillside.

Lennymore, the great wet meadow.

Levencorroch, the rough halfpenny lands.

Locherim Burn, the white or bright water.

Loch na Davie, the loch of the two rivers.

Loch Tanna, the shallow loch.

Machrie, a plain.

Maol Donn, the brown hill.

Meall Biorach, the hill of the heifer.

Meall nan Daimh, the stag hill.

Monamore, the great moor.

Monyquill, the moor or moss of the hazels.

Penrioch (Norse and Gaelic), the brindled pennylands.

Pirnmill. So named from the fact that pirns or spools for cotton were made from the birch which was plentiful in the neighbourhood.

Pladda (Norse), flat island.

Rudha Ban, the white point.

Rudha Glas, the green point.

Rudha Salach, the point of the willow.

Sail Chalmadale, the heel of Saint Calman or Colman.
Scriden (Gaelic *Sgriodan*), a landslip.
Shedog, the windy place.
Shisken, a marsh, quagmire.
Sliddery (Norse), place of swords, or (Gaelic) slaughter.
String (Norse *Strengr*), a cord, road.
Struey, the place of streams.
Suidhe Fhearghas, the seat of Fergus.

Thundergay (Gaelic, *Ton ri gaoith*), haunch to the wind.
Torbeg, the little hill or bleaching green.
Tormore, the great bleaching green.

Whitefarland, the white farthing land.

APPENDIX II

DISTANCES

The following distances are roughly given, and are over rather than under stated.

Brodick to Corrie	5½ miles
Corrie to Sannox	1 "
Sannox to Lochranza (by road)	6½ "
(by shore)	10 "
Lochranza to Pirnmill	6½ "
Pirnmill to Dougrie	5 "
Dougrie to Machrie	2 "
Machrie to Blackwaterfoot	4½ "
Blackwaterfoot to Brodick by The String	10½ "
Blackwaterfoot to Corriecravie	4 "
Bennecarigan Farm to Lamlash by Glen Scorrodale	9 "
Corriecravie to Lagg	2½ "
Lagg to Kildonan	6 "
Kildonan to Whiting Bay	3½ "
Whiting Bay to Lamlash	5 "
Lamlash to Brodick	4 "

WALKS

This list is intended for convenience and easy reference. Most of the walks are fully described in Chapters VI–X. The distances are merely approximations and are given for one direction only.

From Brodick. (1) Up Glen Cloy, to Glen Ormidale or Gleann Dubh beyond (1–3 miles). (2) Up Glen Rosa (2–4 miles). (For crossing of Saddle and ascent of Goatfell, see Chapter IX.) (3) To Corriegills (2 miles). (4) To Corrie by the Shore Road (5½ miles). (5) To Blackwaterfoot by the String (10½ miles).

From Lamlash.—(1) To Clauchlands Point (2½ miles). (2) Up Benlister Glen (1–2 miles). (3) To Brodick by road (4 miles). (4) To Kings Cross Point (3 miles). (5) To Lagg by Monamore Glen and Glen Scorrodale (10 miles).

From Whiting Bay.—(1) To the Golf Course (1 mile). (2) Up Glenashdale Burn to the Waterfalls (2 miles). (3) To Largymore and the Giant's Grave (1½ miles). (4) To Dippin (2½ miles) and Kildonan (1½ miles from Dippin) by road. (5) To Kings Cross Point by the Shore (1½ miles).

From Lochranza.—(1) To Catacol by the Shore Road (1½ miles). (2) To Sannox Bay by road (6½ miles). (3) To Loch na Davie by Gleann Easan Biorach (4 miles). (4) To the Cock of Arran, the Fallen Rocks, and North Sannox by the shore (10 miles in all).

From Corrie.—(1) To Brodick by road (5½ miles). (2) To Sannox (1 mile). (3) To the Fallen Rocks (3½ miles). (4) Up Glen Sannox (3½ miles). (5) To Lochranza (7½ miles).

From Blackwater Foot.—(1) To Drumadoon Point and the King's Cave by the shore (2½ miles). (2) To Machrie (4 miles), and Dougrie (2 miles from Machrie) by road. (3) To Brodick by The String (10½ miles). (4) To Kilpatrick (1½ miles) and Corriecravie (2½ miles from Kilpatrick) by road.

Golf and Fishing

From Lagg.—(1) Up the Kilmory Water (1–3 miles). (2) To Bennan Head and Struey Rocks by the shore (3½ miles). (3) To Levencorroch (3 miles) and Kildonan (3 miles from Levencorroch) by road. (4) To Lamlash by Glen Scorrodale and Monamore Glen (10 miles).

GOLF-COURSES

Brodick.
Sannox (1 mile from Corrie).
Lochranza.
Pirnmill.
Machrie.
Blackwaterfoot.
Corriecravie.
Dippin (between Dippin and Kildonan).
Whiting Bay.
Lamlash.

FISHING

Free fishing is allowed in all rivers except the Machrie and Iorsa and their tributaries. The best of the other streams are Sliddery, Kilmory Water, Rosa, Sannox, and Chalmadale, and the best flies are Teal and Red, Teal and Yellow, Teal and Silver and Blue, Dunkeld, Jungle Cock, Cock-a-Bundy, Grouse and Claret, Butcher, and Woodcock and Yellow.

APPENDIX III

LIST OF PLANTS

The nomenclature in the following list is, so far as possible, in agreement with the latest London catalogue. I wish to state here my indebtedness to Mr. Ian W. Tervet, of Glasgow University, for substantial assistance in compiling this list. It should be noted that the list is arranged according to natural orders, and that the second column gives the localities where the plants may be found.

Thalictrum alpinum ..	Goatfell, head of Glen Sannox, [Ben Bharrain.
— *minus*	Whiting Bay.
— *majus*	
— *flavum*	Whiting Bay.

List of Plants

Ranunculus hederaceus	In many places.
— *Lingua*	Lamlash.
— *acris*	Near Lamlash
— *sceleratus*	
Trollius europæus	
Corydalis claviculata	House roofs and woody places
Cardamine hirsuta	Near Lamlash.
Cochlearia officinalis	On the shores.
— *danica*	
Cakile marita	Frequent on sandy shores.
Lepidium heterophyllum var. *Smithii*	Brodick.
Sisymbrium Sophia	Sandy seashores.
Brassica monensis	Sands at Brodick, Sannox [Blackwaterfoot, &c.
Crambe maritima	Imachar.
Raphanus maritimus	South end.
Helianthemum Chamæcistus	Kildonan.
Viola palustris	Marshy places.
— *tricolor Linn.* var. *arvensis*	
var. *Curtisii*	
Drosera anglica	Frequent.
— *rotundifolia*	Frequent.
Parnassia palustris	Frequent.
Silene maritima	Shores, frequent.
Lychnis dioica	Common.
— *alba*	Common.
— *Githago*	Cornfields, common.
Sagina maritima	On the shores.
— *nodosa*	Lamlash.
Stellaria media	Frequent.
Spergularia salina	On the coast
Radiola linoides	Lochranza.
Althæa officinalis	Struey rocks.
Malva moschata	
Hypericum perforatum	Frequent.
— *dubium*	Invercloy, Whiting Bay, &c., [abundant.
— *Androsæmum*	Frequent in thickets.
— *tetrapterum*	Wet places.
— *humifusum*	Frequent.
— *pulchrum*	Common.

List of Plants

Hypericum hirsutum	Lamlash.
— *elodes*	King's Cave and Lochranza.
Geranium pratense	Brodick, Bennan Head, Holy [Isle, &c.
— *sanguineum*	Strucy, Thundergay, Dippin.
— *dissectum*	Frequent.
— *pusillum*	Frequent.
Trifolium filiforme	
— *medium*	
— *procumbens*	
Anthyllis Vulneraria	Frequent.
Lotus major	Common.
Vicia sylvatica	King's Cave, Kildonan, &c.
— *hirsuta*	
— *Cracca*	Frequent.
— *sepium*	Frequent.
— *lathyroides*	
Lathyrus sylvestris	Strucy rocks.
Geum intermedium, Ehrh.	Frequent.
— *urbanum*	Common.
— *rivale*	Frequent.
Alchemilla vulgaris, Linn.	Common.
— *alpina*	On the mountains.
— *argentea*	Glen Sannox.
— *arvensis*	Frequent.
Agrimonia Eupatoria	On the south coast.
— *odorata*	
Prunus spinosa	
Rosa spinosissima	Frequent.
— *canina*	Common.
— *involuta Sm.*	Lamlash.
— *tomentosa*	Dippin.
— *dumetorum*	
— *Sabina, Woods*	
Pyrus Aucuparia, Ehrh.	Frequent.
Rubus carpinifolius	Lamlash.
— *corylifolius*	Lamlash.
— *Idæus*	Woods and mountains, frequent.
— *saxatilis*	Head of Glen Cloy.
— *suberectus*	Holy Isle and Lamlash.
— *polyanthemus*	
— *villicaulis*	

List of Plants

Rubus rhamnifolius	
Circæa lutetiana	Frequent.
— *alpina*	Benlister Glen, Glen Cloy.
Peplis Portula	
Lythrum Salicaria	Frequent.
Montia fontana	
Scleranthus annuus	In many places
Cotyledon Umbilicus-Veneris	Frequent.
Sedum roseum	Mountains, frequent.
— *Telephium*	A garden escape.
— *acre*	Frequent on the shores.
— *anglicum*	Common.
Saxifraga stellaris	Mountains, frequent.
— *hypnoides*	Glen Cloy, &c.
Hydrocotyle vulgaris	Common.
Æthusa Cynapium	Waste ground.
Sanicula europæa	Thickets.
Eryngium maritimum	Sandy shores.
Conopodium denudatum	Frequent.
Pimpinella Saxifraga	Frequent.
Œnanthe Lachenalii	Corriegills, &c.
Conium maculatum	Dippin, Lagg.
Smyrnium Olusatrum	Dippin.
Scandix Pecten-Veneris	Frequent.
Myrrhis Odorata	Dippin.
Ligusticum scoticum	South end, Kildonan, &c.
Apium graveolens	Shore at Lagg, and Lochranza.
— *nodiflorum*	Shore at Leac a Bhreac.
Galium boreale	Glen Loig, North Sannox, and
Asperula odorata	Woods. [other places.
Valeriana officinalis	Frequent.
Carlina vulgaris	Struey rocks.
Carduus palustris	
Bidens cernua	Brodick.
— *tripartita*	Lamlash.
Eupatorium cannabinum	In many places.
Antennaria dioica	Pastures and moors.
Cichorium Intybus	Whiting Bay.
Gnaphalium uliginosum	Lochranza.
— *sylvaticum*	Lochranza.
Aster Tripolium	Salt marshes.

List of Plants

Hieracium murorum Linn.	Near Lamlash.
— rivale	
— umbellatum	
Filago germanica ..	Brodick, Glen Ashdale.
— minima	Glen Ashdale.
Solidago Virgaurea ..	Glens, frequent.
Senecio sylvaticus ..	Lamlash
Matricaria inodora var. maritima	Sea coast.
Jasione montana	Common.
Lobelia Dortmanna ..	Near Lochranza, Loch Iorsa.
Vaccinium Myrtillus ..	Frequent.
— Vitis-Idæa	On the higher mountains.
Arctostaphylos alpina ..	Holy Isle, Glen Easan Bhiorach
Pyrola minor	Holy Isle.
Ilex Aquifolium	On the rocks.
Fraxinus excelsior ..	Rocks at Glen Catacol.
Erythræa Centaurium ..	Frequent.
— compressa	Shore at Corriegills, &c
Gentiana campestris ..	Moors and pastures.
Menyanthes trifoliata ..	Springbank, &c.
Convolvulus arvensis ..	Corrie.
Calystegia sepium ..	Hedges, frequent.
— Soldanella	Blackwaterfoot.
Lithospermum officinale ..	Lochranza.
Solanum Dulcamara ..	Brodick, Holy Isle, &c.
Veronica montana ..	Blue Rock, and woods in other [places.
— polita	
Melampyrum pratense ..	Abundant.
Scrophularia aquatica ..	Near Sannox.
Digitalis purpurea ..	Frequent.
Linaria vulgaris	
Verbascum Thapsus ..	Cliffs at Struey and Dippin.
Lycopus europæus ..	Sannox.
Mentha alopecuroides	
— viridis	Near Corrie.
— rotundifolia	Brodick (garden outcast).
Galeopsis speciosa ..	Frequent.
Lamium amplexicaule ..	Lochranza.
— mollucellifolium ..	Lamlash, Kildonan, Machrie, [&c.
Stachys ambigua, Sm. ..	Sliddery.
Scutellaria galericulata ..	Brodick, Struey, &c.

List of Plants

Scutellaria minor	
Pinguicula vulgaris ..	Abundant.
— *lusitanica*	In the bogs, less frequent than
	[formerly.
Utricularia vulgaris ..	Loch na Davie, Loch Iorsa.
— *minor*	Loch on the shore, near
— *intermedia*	[Machrie.
Glaux maritima	Salt marshes.
Anagallis arvensis ..	In cultivated ground.
— *tenella*	Abundant in the bogs.
Centunculus minimus	
Samolus Valerandi ..	Marshes, frequent.
Armeria maritima ..	Seashore, abundant.
Littorella uniflora ..	Lochranza.
Plantago maritima ..	On the shores.
— *Coronopus*	Dry places.
Atriplex maritima ..	Sea shores.
— *patula*	Shore at Struey.
— — (*var. erecta*) ..	Sliddery.
— *glabriuscula var. virescens*	
Salicornia herbacea, Linn.	Lochranza.
Suæda maritima	On the shores, Lochranza, &c.
Salsola Kali	Sandy shores, frequent.
Rumex glomeratus	
Polygonum Raii	Shore at Lamlash, Lagg, &c.
— *Convolvulus*	On the shores.
— *aviculare Linn.*	
Oxyria digyna	Mountains.
Empetrum nigrum ..	Lagg.
Parietaria ramiflore ..	Brodick Castle.
Ulmus montana	
Myrica Gale	Abundant.
Betula alba	Frequent.
Salix herbacea	Mountain tops.
Corylus Avellana ..	Abundant.
Populas tremula	Torlin.
— *alba*	
Juniperus communis ..	Mountains.
— *siberica*	Goatfell (?) [Bay.
Cephalanthera ensifolia ..	Sliddery, Invercloy, Whiting
Listera ovata	Lamlash. [Glen Cloy.
— *cordata*	Cir Mhor, Suidhe Fhearghas,

List of Plants

Orchis mascula	Abundant.
— *Fuchsii*	Abundant.
— *latifolia*	Abundant.
Platanthera bifolia	Abundant.
— *chlorantha*	
Cœloglossum viride	Whitefarland, Eas-a-mhor, Lochranza.
Leuchorchis albida	Lochranza; and dry heaths in many places.
Gymnadenia conopsea	Abundant in fields and heather.
Malaxis paludosa	Kildonan.
Allium ursinum	Abundant.
— *vineale*	
Juncus triglumis	Goatfell.
— *trifidus*	Goatfell.
— *Gerardi*	Salt marshes.
— *inflexus*	Torlin.
— *maritimus*	Sea shores.
Narthecium ossifragum	Abundant.
Alisma Plantago-aquatica	Brodick, &c.
— *ranunculoides*	In several places.
Triglochin palustre	Frequent.
— *maritimum*	Salt marshes.
Typha latifolia	Mill-dam, Whiting Bay, &c.
Sparganium ramosum	Lamlash.
— *simplex*	
Potamegeton coloratus	
— *nitens*	
Zostera marina	Abundant.
Eriophorum vaginatum	Goatfell.
— *angustifolium*	Abundant.
Schoenus nigricans	Sea shores.
Eleocharis palustris	Sea shores.
uniglumis	Sands near Kildonan, and at Lagg
— *multicaulis*	On the coast.
Scirpus rufus	On the seashore.
— *compressus*	On the seashore.
Scirpus maritimus	On the seashore.
— *pauciflorus*	Corriegills and Corrie shore.
Carex inflatus	Near Machrie.
— *helodes*	Roadside between Brodick and Lamlash; Lochranza, Corriegills.

Carex vulpina	Shores.
— *pauciflora*	Ascent of Goatfell, and in Glen [Rosa.
— *remota*	
— *canescens*	On the moors.
— *distans*	Imachar.
— *extensa*	
— *fulva*	
— *pilulifera*	
— *Œderi*	Near Dougrie.
— *rigida*	Goatfell.
Rhyncospora alba	North Glen Sannox, &c.
Scirpus setaceus	Frequent.
Ammophila arundinacea	On the shores.
Elymus arenarius	Sandy shores.
Briza media	
Deschampsia alpina	Goatfell.
Brachypodium sylvaticum	Woods.
Catabrosa aquatica	Shore at Kildonan and Lagg.
Festuca rottbœllioides	
Bromus gigantea	Corriegills.
Molinia cœrulea	On the mountains.
Agropyron junceum	Shore at Sliddery.
Polypodium vulgare	Very common.
Phegopteris polypodioides	Abundant in the woods, and along the sea cliffs; frequent also in sheltered spots in the glens, and sometimes found in rock crevices at the top of the highest mountains.
— *Dryopteris*	In the woods, and very abundant in damp sheltered spots in the glens and among the heather; often ascending the highest mountains along with the last species.
Polystichum aculeatum	Frequent on cliffs and banks near the sea.
Lastrea spinulosa	Very abundant in several varieties.
— *montana*	Very abundant in the glens and on the moors, often, as in the lower part of Glen Rosa,

	covering the whole hillside with the delicate yellowish-green of its fronds.
Lastrea Filix mas ..	Abundant everywhere.
— *aristata* ..	Frequent on the sea cliff, as at Corrie, North Sannox, Saltpans, and Whiting Bay; in rocky and wooded ground at the head of Glen Cloy.
— — *var. dumetorum*	
— — *collina*	
— — *alpina*	
Cystopteris fragilis ..	Rocks at the head of Glen Cloy, near Glen Sannox, and in several spots among the mountains. It generally, if not always, occurs in the form *dentata*.
Asplenium Ruta-muraria	Old walls at Brodick Castle, and probably in other places.
— *Trichomanes*	Common on rocks and walls.
— *viride*	Abundant on limestone cliffs at the head of Benlister Glen, above Lamlash; on the rocks near the head of Glen Cloy, sparingly.
— *marinum*	Occurring here and there in caves along the old sea cliff. Scarcely to be found on the east and north coasts, but may be obtained in many places on the south and west.
— *Adiantum-nigrum* ..	Abundant on rocks and banks.
Athyrium Filix-fœmina ..	Very abundant and beautiful.
— — *var. incisum* ..	Corrie.
Phyllitis Scolopendrium	Hedges, banks, and rocks; often [very luxuriant.
Pteris aquilina	Common.
Cryptogramme crispa ..	Among granite blocks at the head of Glen Sannox, under the crags of Cir Mhor, abundant, and in small quantities elsewhere.
Blechnum spicant ..	Common.
Botrychium Lunaria ..	Fields near The String in Glen Shirag; also on the shore at

Invercloy and Corriegills, and in dry pastures elsewhere.

Trichomanes radicans .. In moist cliffs near Corrie, and near Machrie Bay, in very small quantities. ("That rare and extremely beautiful filmy fern, which occurs in a few places in the wet, shady recesses of rocks near the Lakes of Killarney, in North Wales, and in the Isle of Arran. Elsewhere it is found only in the Azores, The Canary Islands, and in the island of Madeira".)

Hymenophyllum tunbridgense Upon the old sea cliff in several places, as in a plantation near Invercloy, in the wood at Brodick Castle, near Corrie, at Fallen Rocks, and at the entrance of Glen Ashdale.

Hymenophyllum peltatum Abundant in many spots, as near Corrie; sea coast at Sannox; Glen Cloy; Benlister Glen; Birk Glen, above Invercloy, often growing with the last-mentioned species, but also ascending to the tops of the highest mountains, where, as on Ben Nuis, it covers the most exposed rocks at a height of 2500 feet, and is with difficulty distinguished from a moss. In general it prefers damper spots than *H. tunbridgense.*

Osmunda regalis .. .. Once frequent on the sea cliff all round the island, often very luxuriant, attaining the height of 10 or even 12 feet. Now less abundant than formerly, but may be found near

	Lochranza, and at King's Cave.
Ophioglossum vulgatum ..	In a meadow between Bennan Head and Torlin, and probably in other places.
Lycopodium clavatum ..	Abundant on the hills.
— *Selago*	Moors and mountains, frequent.
— *annotinum*	Said to have been found on
— *alpinum*	On the mountains. [Goatfell.
Equisetum variegatum	
— *arvense*	Common.
— *sylvaticum*	In the woods and glens, not in-
— *limosum*	Ditches and ponds. [frequent.
— *palustre*	Boggy places.

BIBLIOGRAPHY

TOPOGRAPHY, POPULATION, &c., (Chapter I)

Ordnance Gazeteer of Scotland.
New Statistical Account of Scotland: Buteshire.
Ordnance Survey Map of Scotland: Isle of Arran.
Macnair: *Argyllshire and Buteshire* (*Cambridge County Geographies*).
Landsborough: *Arran: Its Topography, Natural History, &c.*
Census of Scotland, 1931: *County of Bute.*
Report of the Departmental Committee on Tinkers in Scotland.

GEOLOGY (Chapter II)

Tyrrell: *The Geology of Arran* (*Memoirs of the Geological Survey*).
Bryce: *The Geology of Arran and Clydesdale.*
The Book of Arran: The Building-up of the Island, by Sir A. Geikie.
Ramsay: *Geology of the Island of Arran.*
Geological Map of Arran.
Fauna, Flora, and Geology of the Clyde Area (British Association).
Ordnance Gazeteer of Scotland: The Geology of Scotland, by Peach and Horne.
Holmes: *The Age of the Earth.*

ARCHÆOLOGY (Chapter III)

The Book of Arran.
Mitchell and Kennedy: *Prehistoric Man in Scotland* (*Chambers's Journal* for Jan., June, and Oct., 1932).

Bibliography

Macalister: *The Archæology of Ireland.*
Perry: *The Growth of Civilization.*
Peake and Fleure: *The Corridors of Time.*

HISTORY (Chapter IV)

The Book of Arran.
Bremner: *The Norsemen in Alban.*
Mawer: *The Vikings.*
Johnstone: *The Norwegian Account of King Haco's Expedition.*
Cameron: *The Church in Arran.*

NATURAL HISTORY (Chapter XI)

The Fauna, Flora, and Geology of the Clyde Area. (British Association).
Step: *Animal Life of the British Isles.*
Cameron: *The Wild Red Deer of Scotland.*
Jenkins: *The Fishes of the British Isles.*
Bryce: *The Geology of Arran.*
Landsborough: *Arran and its Natural History.*

ORNITHOLOGY (Chapter XII)

Baxter and Rintoul: *The Geographical Distribution and Status of Birds in Scotland.*
McWilliam: *The Birds of the Island of Bute.*
Paton and Pike: *The Birds of Ayrshire.*
Massingham: *Birds of the Seashore.*

BOTANY (Chapter XIII)

Bryce: *The Flora of the Island of Arran.*
Fauna, Flora, and Geology of the Clyde Area (British Association).

PLACE-NAMES (Appendix I)

Currie: *The Place-Names of Arran.*

INDEX

A' Chir, 101–2.
Adders, 116.
Alltgobhlach, 69.
Am Binnein, 2, 59.
Arran: archæology of, 20.
— climate of, 6–7.
— fauna of, 111.
— flora of, 133.
— geography of, 1.
— geology of, 11.
— history of, 34.
— population of, 8–9.
Auchangallon, 30.
Auchmore, 69.

Baker, E. A., 107.
Balliekine, 8, 69.
Ballymichael, 73.
Barytes, 63.
Ben Bharrain, 2, 91, 98.
Ben Bhreac, 2, 90.
Ben Chliabhain, 2, 4, 87, 107.
Bennan Head, 76.
Ben Nuis, 2, 4, 107–110.
Ben Tarsuinn, 2, 98, 107.
Blackwaterfoot, 30, 70, 73.
Book of Arran, The, 4, 21, 73.
Bowmen's Pass, 98, 107.
Brodick, 46, 48, 54, 61.
Brodick Castle, 41, 43, 44, 56–7.
Bronze Age, 28.
Bruce, King Robert, 40.
Bryce, James, 11, 29, 86, 117, 133.
Bryce, James, Viscount Bryce, 133.
Burican, 75.
Burrel, John, 45.
Bute, County of, 1.

Caisteal Abhail, 2, 88 ff., 98 102.
Carlin's Leap, 17, 88, 98, 102.
Carn Ban, 21.
Castles, the, 2, 88 ff., 98, 102.
Catacol Bay, 66.
Cat Stone, the, 61, 101.
Ceum na Caillich, 17, 88, 98, 102.
Cioch na h-Oighe, 2, 61, 97, 103–4, 115.
Cir Mhor, 2, 87, 88 ff., 97, 103–7.

Index

Clachaig, Cairn at, 29, 67.
Clach Mhor, 59, 101.
Clauchlands Point, 81.
Climate of Arran, 6–7.
Cnoc Dubh, 89.
Cock of Arran, 13, 14, 64.
Coire a' Bhradain, 89.
Coire Daingean, 98, 102, 107.
Coirein Lochain, 68, 90.
Columba, 35, 76.
Corrie, 14, 15, 44, 59, 60.
Corriecravie, 32, 75.
Corriegills, 141.

Deer, 112.
Devil's Punchbowl, 89, 97, 103, 130.
Dippin, 78.
Dougrie, 13, 69, 91.
Drumadoon, 33, 36, 67, 70, 71.
Dunan Beag, 24, 25, 26, 29, 31.
— Mor, 24, 25, 29.

Ettrick Shepherd (quoted), 63.

Fallen Rocks, 13, 19, 64, 90.
Fingal, 66.
Fishing in Arran, 5.
Fullarton Family, 42.

Gaelic names, pronunciation of, 4, 143.
Garbh Allt, 87, 89.
Giants' Graves, 22, 25, 79.
Gleann Dubh, 32, 55, 89.
Glen Ashdale, 5, 79.
Glen Catacol, 66, 90.
Glen Chalmadale, 5, 64.
Glen Cloy, 5, 8, 32, 41, 55, 89.
Glencloy Fort, 32.
Glen Easan Biorach, 5, 89, 91.
Glen Iorsa, 2, 5, 16.
Glen Ormidale, 55, 89.
Glen Rosa, 2, 4, 5, 8, 55, 86, 87.
Glen Sannox, 2, 5, 8, 13, 32, 62, 64, 88, 90, 97.
Glen Scorrodale, 5, 6, 75.
Glen Shant, 86.
Glen Shurig, 5, 74.
Goatfell, 2, 47, 92–6.

Hamilton Family, the, 43–4, 81.
Hamilton Rock, 81.
Headrick (quoted), 45.
Holy Isle, 32, 36, 37, 82–4.

Imachar, 5, 69.
Iorsa Water, 5, 69, 90, 91.
Ireland, 1, 26, 27, 30, 31, 34.

Keats (quoted), 47.
Kilbrannan Sound, 35.
Kilbride, parish of, 2.
Kildonan, 61, 78.
Kilmichael, the Fullartons and, 42.

Index

Kilmory, parish of, 2.
Kilpatrick, 36, 74.
King's Cave, 70, 71.
Kings Cross Point, 32, 38, 79.
Knockenkelly, 79.

Lagg, 61, 75.
Lamlash, 48, 61, 80.
Landsborough (quoted), 54, 80, 117.
Lennymore, 68.
Levencorroch, 76.
Lithgow, Wm. (quoted), 57.
Loch na Davie, 89.
Lochranza, 5, 65, 90.
Loch Tanna, 91.

Macdonald, Hugh (quoted), 130.
Machrie, 60, 69.
Machrie Moor, 30, 67, 69.
Machrie Water, 5, 15, 70.
McKirdy, 77–8.
Meall Biorach, 90.
Meall Breac, 59.
Meall nan Damh, 68, 90.
Mitchell, W. (quoted), 46.
Moinechoill Cairn, 23.
Monamore Chamber, 23.
Monamore Glen, 79.
Montrose Family, 46.
Mountains of Arran, 2, 85–110.

Newton Point, 65.
North Sannox, 64.

Ossian, 66.
Ossian's Mound, 29.

Penrioch, 69.
Pirnmill, 60, 69, 145.
Pladda, 76.

Ramsay, Sir Andrew C. (quoted), 68.
Red Deer, 112.
Rocking Stone, 62, 101.

Saddle, the, 2, 87, 97.
St. Brendan, 35, 74.
St. Columba, 35, 76.
St. Molios, 36, 73.
St. Molios's Cave, 32, 39, 82.
Sannox, 24, 32, 61, 90.
Scriden, 19, 65.
Seals, 118.
Sgiath Bhan, 89.
Sharks, 118–9.
Shiskine, 73.
Sliddery, 75.
Smuggling, 72, 77.
Stacach, the, 59, 96.
String, the, 5, 55, 73, 86.
Stronach Ridge, 33.
Struey Rocks, 76.
Suidhe Fhearghas, 2, 88, 98.

Thundergay, 68.
Tinkers, 10.

Index

Torlin Cairn, 22, 26.
Tormore, 70.
Tormore Cairn, 24.
Tormore Chambers, 23.
Tormore Moss, 33.

Vikings and Viking Graves, 37–40.

Waddell, P. Hately (quoted), 67.
Whales, 118.
Whisky, 72.
Whitefarland, 69, 91.
White Water, 59.
Whiting Bay, 48, 49, 61, 79.
Wordsworth (quoted), 48.